P9-CKT-370

(Continued from front flap)

Here is the story of Enrico Caruso's 1910 maiden broadcast and the uniformly bad press it drew.

Here, too, is the story—as opposed to the legend—of David Sarnoff, whose promotion of the "Radio Music Box" transformed the nation's domestic life and created the giant we know as RCA.

Here is Herbert Hoover, then Secretary of Commerce, who more than anyone else shaped the government's controversial role in regulating radio.

Here are the brightest stars of the burgeoning medium: Vincent Lopez, radio's first and most durable popular music attraction; "Vic and Sade"; announcers Graham McNamee, Ted Husing, Jimmy Wallington, Clem McCarthy, and Herb Morrison, who pierced a nation's heart with his firsthand account of the *Hindenburg* disaster.

Here are FDR and Arthur Godfrey, Fred Allen and Jack Benny, Bob Hope and Lester Kroll (radio's "Mr. Anthony"). Here is Will Rogers, who said, "Radio is too big a thing to be out of!" and William Paley, whose CBS fought the battle for bigness with Bing Crosby, Amos 'n' Andy, and Al Jolson.

And here is Phillips H. Lord of "Seth Parker" and "Gangbusters" fame, who, if he hadn't really existed, would have had to be invented.

SAM J. SLATE

JOE COOK

Authors SAM J. SLATE and JOE COOK brought more than fifty years' combin[ed] experience in radio to their writing of *It Sounds Impossible*. Slate, a newsm[an] writer, director, and producer, is Vice-President of CBS Radio and Gene[ral] Manager of station WCBS. Joe Cook, who has written and produced many [of] network TV and radio shows, is Program Director for WCBS.

It Sounds Impossible

Hot diggity!
This was a specially posed "cheesecake" picture released
in 1923 by KDKA, Pittsburgh,
to push the excitement, glamour,
and portability of radio.

It Sounds

Impossible

SAM J. SLATE *and* JOE COOK

The Macmillan Company, New York
Collier-Macmillan Limited, London

The authors wish to thank Famous Music Corporation for permission to quote from the composition "Moon River" by Johnny Mercer and Henry Mancini, copyright © 1961 by Famous Music Corporation; and Rand McNally & Company for permission to reprint "When Seth Parker's on the Air" from *Seth Parker Fireside Poems*.

© Sam J. Slate and Joe Cook 1963

All rights reserved—no part of this book may be reproduced in any form without permission in writing from the publisher, except by a reviewer who wishes to quote brief passages in connection with a review written for inclusion in magazine or newspaper.

First Printing

Printed in the United States of America

The Macmillan Company, New York

Collier-Macmillan Canada, Ltd., Toronto, Ontario

Library of Congress catalog card number: 63-14530

The late Dr. Frank Conrad conducted the experimental work that led to the establishment of KDKA Radio and supervised the construction of the station. KDKA began broadcasting on November 2, 1920, with the Harding-Cox election returns.

Acknowledgments

Our sincere thanks to those in broadcasting who gave so generously of their time to afford us firsthand accounts of the formative days of our industry.

To John Royal, Vice President, the National Broadcasting Company, the dean of all big-time broadcasters.

To Vincent Lopez, for his graphic description of the first dance-band remote in 1921.

To Bill Munday, one of the first of America's great sports announcers, who is still doing color for the University of Georgia football games.

To Jimmy Wallington, who made radio announcing a glamorous field, for his recollections of the days of the twenties and thirties, and of the Eddie Cantor, Rudy Vallee, and Major Bowes shows.

To Max Wylie, of the Lennen and Newell Advertising Agency, a student of mass media, producer, director, and writer who contributed many outstanding programs to radio's Golden Age.

To Fran Carlon, Casey Allen, Paul McGrath, Claudia Morgan, Art Hanna, Kay Campbell, and Bill Adams, representatives of a great era of a forgotten art—radio acting.

Acknowledgments

To Robert Trout, of CBS, for his description of radio's finest hour.

To Bert Parks for the greatest line in the book.

To our associates at CBS—Arthur Hull Hayes, President of the Columbia Radio Division; James Seward, Executive Vice President; Fred Ruegg, Vice President of Station Administration—for being kind enough to listen to our long dissertations about this book and for suggesting certain points.

To E. Kidder Meade, Vice President of CBS Corporate Information, who fought his way through the first draft and came up smiling.

To Dave Partridge, National Advertising and Sales Promotion Manager of the Westinghouse Group, for the KDKA Story.

To Stephen B. Labunski, Vice President and General Manager of WMCA, New York; Jerry Danzig, Radio-TV Director for Governor Nelson Rockefeller; Lanny Ross, one of radio's all-time great singing stars; William McCaffrey, New York advertising executive and proprietor of the agency of the same name, for thoughtful consultation.

To Bill Randle for his cogent ideas about radio's worst hour.

To Mildred Joy and Eileen Dwyer, Librarian and Assistant Librarian, respectively, of NBC, who opened their files to make available material that authenticates many of the events in this book.

To Felice Marlier, of CBS Special Projects, without whose untiring efforts we would probably still be typing the manuscript.

To pretty, patient Betty Angelillis, as loyal a secretary as ever suffered through a project such as this.

Our thanks, especially, to Dr. Henry David, President of the New School for Social Research in New York City, who suggested this project in the first place.

Picture Credits

The gallery of photographs in this book was made possible by our good friend and associate, Walter Seigal, Manager, Photo Department, Columbia Broadcasting System. "Izzy's" files provided many hours of nostalgic pleasure. We wish only that we could have included the hundreds and hundreds of rare prints that have been so carefully kept by Mr. Seigal. The KDKA photographs are by courtesy of the Westinghouse Broadcasting Company.

*"The first full-time radio
announcer in the world" is the title
KDKA gave Harold W. Arlin,
shown here in the early 1920's.
He did the first play-by-play football game
and introduced many noted personalities
in their radio debuts on the Pittsburgh station.
Today he is Industrial Relations Manager
for Westinghouse Electric in Mansfield, Ohio.*

Admiral Richard Byrd, shown here with broadcaster Charles Murphy, gave early radio great excitement, and proved the medium had an immediacy that the press could never attain. Both NBC and CBS gave the Little America venture plenty of coverage.

"Radio is too big a thing to be out of,"
said Will Rogers after his debut on NBC.
He used an alarm clock to time his radio comments.
Here, in a picture taken in the early thirties,
he hands the timepiece to Charles Winninger—
then "Cap'n Henry" of the famous
"Showboat" series.

One of the truly big stars in radio's infancy was singer *Ruth Etting,* shown in this tricky publicity shot with orchestra conductor *Lennie Hayton.*

President Calvin Coolidge wouldn't
be disturbed when "Amos 'n' Andy" came on.
Freeman Gosden (left) and Charles Correll
captivated the nation with such
characters as "de Kingfish," "Madame Queen,"
"Lightnin'," and "Henry Van Porter."
They celebrated their thirtieth
year on the air in 1958 (below).

"The Songbird of the South," Kate Smith, opened every show with the first eight bars of "When the Moon Comes Over the Mountain," and her "Hello, Everybody!" became so popular Hollywood starred her in a picture with that title.

*Elvis wasn't first
with sideburns for singers.
This was Crosby's idea of
the "crooner image"
in 1934.*

*Bing's beginnings were with
Paul Whiteman's Rhythm Boys.
He became a single
shortly afterward.*

Rudy Vallee had taken an unknown violinist
by the name of Rubinoff under his wing
and made up a "package" called "Dave Rubinoff and His Orchestra."
The sponsor liked the music and signed
Maurice Chevalier to star. After twenty-six weeks
Chevalier went back to France, and the show
became "The Eddie Cantor Hour."
Rubinoff and his violin became a Sunday-night treat.

The Brooklyn Eagle's *H. V. Kaltenborn (center, standing) became
a CBS news analyst with a program called
"We Look at the World"—later known as
"Kaltenborn Edits the News." Later,
his overseas reporting prior to and during World War II
made him the dean of news commentators. Note the old carbon mike
used during one of his first broadcasts.*

Stoopnagle and Budd (Budd's on the left, center) called themselves "The Gloomchasers." The pair was radio's first utterly daffy two-act. Fred Allen called Stoopnagle "the titan of trivia." Stoop and Budd stayed away from conventional humor, and offered listeners such inventions as upside-down lighthouses for submarines and red, white, and blue starch for people who want stiff flags.

Radio's first popular singing sister act,
The Boswell Sisters,
were heard often on their own program,
and guest-starred with other personalities
such as Bing Crosby, Paul Whiteman,
and Rudy Vallee. They were featured in
films, too. Connee—in the center with
Bing—went on as a single
when her two sisters retired.

Benny Goodman became "The King of Swing"
in the 1930's, and all networks at some time
or other carried his music on dance remotes.
Here is a 1938 rehearsal shot of Goodman with
members of his trio—Lionel Hampton
and Teddy Wilson. On his NBC
"Saturday Night Dance Party" for Kraft,
he shared billing with another newcomer
with a big band—Xavier Cugat.

"Easy Aces" contained some of the best humor
on the air. Jane (left) and Goodman Ace are in
rehearsal in this 1933 picture.
Lines like Jane's, "A person just can't run around
half-crocked buying every little trinket
and junket that comes into her mind!"
made the program a great favorite. "Goody" is now
TV's highest paid scripter.

_dy Vallee started the "guest star" policy
his "Fleischmann's Yeast Hour" in the thirties.
_her shows were quick to adopt the practice,
_h as "The Studebaker Hour," in rehearsal above,
_th guests Helen Morgan and nightclub
r Harry Richman (far right).

"Say good night, Gracie!" George Burns and Gracie Allen
had their own radio show by the time
this 1934 photo was taken in the
New York studios of CBS.

"Only genuine Wrigley's has the green sp
on the pack!" Instead of organ mu
to sign off the story line at
most exciting point, "Myrt and Marge" u
an exploding commercial announce
"Myrt" was Myrtle Vail a
"Marge" was Dora Damerel. The show was anoti
quarter-hour five-a-week favorite
but not a soap opera in the true ser

John Barrymore and Elaine Barry.
"When Barrymore's voice filled the room,"
said NBC program boss John Royal,
"it was the kind of dramatic dynamite
that made showmen weep with appreciation."

Ventriloquism was once considered an impossible act for radio
because listeners couldn't see the dummy.
Then Edgar Bergen did a guest shot on the Rudy Vallee show
with his sidekick Charlie McCarthy.
He was a radio sensation
and was given his own Sunday-night show.
Charlie's "I'll murder ya, so help me;
I'll mow ya down!" swept the nation.

y friends . . ." Franklin D. Roosevelt was the first
sident of the United States to make radio really work for him.
ile still Governor of New York, he wrote,
ime after time in meeting legislative opposition,
ave taken the issue directly to the voters by radio
l invariably I have met a most heartening response."
"Fireside Chats" became
owerful arm of the government.

In his Easter bonnet on a dark Sunday in March of 1937, Bob Trout covers the New York Easter Parade for CBS with a then newfangled wrist microphone, a smart leather shortwave transmitter pack, and a "hot" cane. The cravat, morning coat, and spats made him the best-dressed newscaster on the air. And all before television.

Columbia's "umbrella man" here is Sportscaster Ted Husing broadcasting a golf tournament in 1937. A portable transmitter was fastened to the pole along with binoculars and a microphone. The unit attracted a lot of attention— especially in high winds.

News commentator Boake Carter was an air personality of such magnitude that CBS made it possible for him to broadcast his network program from his Philadelphia home—the ultimate in special privilege in 1938. Carter was one of the first to explain the news in depth.

The nation fell in love with two youngsters whom Eddie Cantor discovered and introduced on his radio show. Bobby Breen and Deanna Durbin are pictured here with Eddie during the rehearsal of his 1937 Christmas show.

Chet Lauck (left) and Norris (Toughie) Goff were radio's beloved Lum 'n' Abner. Their adventures in the rural Jot 'Em Down Store were always funny—often hilarious. (Below) In costume for the "Lum 'n' Abner" motion-picture series. There always seemed to be a dog around in their picture sessions (1938 photograph).

One October night in 1938 Orson Welles broadcast
the Mercury Theatre production of "War of the Worlds,"
and the eastern seaboard was thrown into panic—
many believing the world was being invaded from Mars.
Welles "hid out" from the press in a CBS studio that night.
The next morning every newspaper and newsreel camera company
wanted pictures and statements.
Welles met them all in a CBS studio at noon.

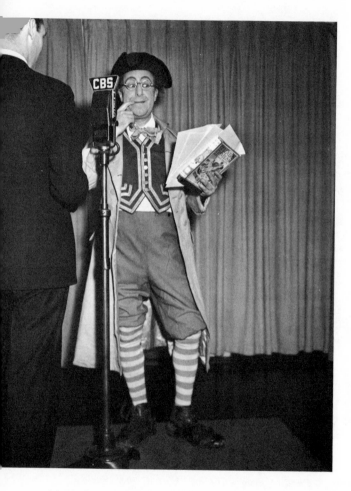

It wasn't uncommon in radio's golden age
for a star such as Ed Wynn
to appear at his broadcasts in costume.
It often gave the comedian a better "feel" of his character,
and certainly helped get lively response from the studio audience.

Molly Berg's radio "family" looked like this in 1939.
"The Goldbergs" was a warm, human
quarter-hour program that Molly wrote and starred in.
Recognize the man second from the right?
That's film and TV star Everett Sloane.

The residents of "the little house halfway up in the next block"—
Vic and Sade—played by Art Van Harvey and Bernadine Flynn.
Writer Paul Rymer had a great ear for the talk habits of middle-
class Midwesterners, and it was one of the funniest yet most heartwarming serials on the air. Their world contained a son, Rush, a
neighbor boy named Blue Tooth Johnson, a garbage man named
Mr. Gumpox, and a relative named Uncle Fletcher. Sade and her
friend, Ruthie, never missed a washrag sale at Yamleton's Department Store.

*The newscaster was to become the star
of radio when World War II erupted.
The soon-to-be-big names on the CBS news team in 1939
were (left to right) Edward R. Murrow,
Paul White, news director; Maurice Hindus,
Robert Trout, and H. V. Kaltenborn.*

Fred Allen and his wife, Portland Hoffa,
at the peak of their show's success . . . in the forties.
Allen wasn't an instant hit on radio,
but his barbed wit eventually made him
one of its most popular entertainers.

S' *Director of News, the late Paul White*
his famous "piano"—the switching board
his desk that allowed him to talk to any correspondent
place in the world where CBS could string
ne or set up a transmitter.
s "electric brain" helped him administrate
umbia's tremendous coverage of World War II.

PREFACE

A MAN about 46 years of age, giving the name of Joshua Coppersmith, has been arrested in New York for attempting to extort funds from ignorant and superstitious people by exhibiting a device which he says will convey the human voice any distance over metallic wires so that it will be heard by the listener at the other end. He calls the instrument a "telephone," which is obviously intended to imitate the word "telegraph" and win the confidence of those who know the success of the latter instrument without understanding the principles on which it is based.

Well informed people know that it is impossible to transmit the human voice over wires as may be done with dots and dashes and signals of the Morse code, and that, were it possible to do so, the thing would be of no practical value. The authorities who apprehended this criminal are to be congratulated, and it is hoped this punishment will be prompt and fitting.

From an 1872 Boston newspaper clipping—
VINCENT LOPEZ COLLECTION.

Preface

It sounded impossible to proper Bostonians in 1872, and even today, some ninety-five years later, much of the story of broadcasting reads like a fantasy.

This book about the huge, diversified industry poses the obvious question What kind of book? This isn't a textbook for students. It isn't an all-inclusive, comprehensive history of the birth and chronological development of radio; yet it is, in a way, a documented study of the social and economic impact of broadcasting on the twentieth century.

It will be, we hope, an amusing, interesting commentary that will give you a better understanding and appreciation of this amazing business.

Sam J. Slate and Joe Cook, the writers, have, between them, spent some fifty years in broadcasting. Their paths and backgrounds were quite dissimilar except that along the way both had been writers for the networks. Cook's work has been comedy and variety, while Slate's was dramatic and documentary.

Cook began his broadcasting career at KDAL, Duluth, Minnesota, then went to KSTP in Minneapolis. A few years later the National Broadcasting Company moved him to New York to head broadcast promotion for the television network. During his NBC days he pounded out over a thousand radio and TV scripts for such diverse bosses as Bert Parks, Tony Bennett, Jaye P. Morgan, Walter O'Keefe, Pat Carroll, Margaret Truman, Mike Wallace, Arnold Stang, Martha Scott, and Paul Winchell and Jerry Mahoney. Cook now has an executive post with the Columbia Broadcasting System, and continues to write nights and weekends or whenever he has the time and inclination.

Slate, with several years' experience as a newspaper

reporter in the South, began his broadcasting experience in New York nearly thirty years ago. He's been a newsman, writer, director, producer, program executive, and now he's a vice president of CBS Radio and general manager of the network's key station, WCBS, New York. In the years of World War II he traveled over 100,000 miles writing such programs as "Defense for America" for NBC and "This Nation at War" for The American Broadcasting Company. They were among the first of the big network documentaries. Just after the war he was named program director of the British Broadcasting Corporation's New York office—a post he held for six years. Slate has spent much time abroad, and is knowledgeable about European broadcasting.

In this book Slate and Cook will share with you some of their varied experiences and specialized knowledge, and introduce you to many of their friends and colleagues, who will contribute a point of view, a memory, or a laugh.

At times, which will be clearly identified, they shall write in the first person. This they've found necessary, as many of their experiences are so different, and so separated by time and geography, that concerted collaboration was impractical.

But before we populate our story with the warm, living people around us, let's look at the very beginning.

In the twentieth century four industrial developments greatly altered the way and concept of human life—more so than any other inventions or discoveries since fire and the wheel. They were the automobile, the airplane, the telephone—and broadcasting. Even in the age of wonder drugs and atomic sciences, people have not felt such a tremendous impact or completeness of change at both the social and economic levels as was brought about in so short a time by these four inventions.

Of the four, broadcasting reached deep into mores, manners, and modes so quickly that, nearly overnight, it changed the table conversations, the recreation habits, the manner of speaking, the musical tastes, the appetite for information, the shopping and even the sleeping habits of the entire world. Its forcefulness changed all of show business. Its immediacy shortened the day and shrank the globe.

The complex radio and television industry is not a story of a single road of development. Hundreds of inventors and inventions were involved.

Three hundred years before Christ the Greeks had a telegraph system of sorts—sending the alphabet through the air from hill to hill by means of torches.

France had semaphore signaling as early as the eighteenth century.

An Italian philosopher by the name of Giambattista della Porta suggested, in 1569, that a signal might be sent electrically with a pair of magnetic compasses.

Benjamin Franklin—with his kite—made a big contribution to the future business of broadcasting when he showed that the flash of an electric spark from one wire to another was similar to a lightning flash from a cloud to the earth. He believed the speed of electricity to be—in his word—"inconceivable."

Samuel Morse, in the early 1830's, with a series of batteries and coils was able to send a message through two hundred feet of wire.

The development of alternators and generators pushed

the possibility of a wireless system along—here was electrical force harnessed in a usable form.

Of course, Dr. Alexander Graham Bell's invention advanced the wonders of radio and television when, in 1875, while working on a telegraphic device for reproducing sound, he accidentally stumbled on a secret of transmitting the human voice electrically.

If it's a matter of keeping the credits straight, Roger Bacon probably started the whole thing back in 1262 when he was fooling around with the idea of using electricity for communication.

Too, we must consider the case of Nat Stubblefield. You never heard of Stubblefield? Nathan B. Stubblefield, in 1892, nine years before Marconi sent his first wireless signal across the Atlantic, figured out a way to transmit the human voice through the air. He waited until 1902 to demonstrate it publicly. On New Year's Day, 1902, in Fairmont Park, Philadelphia, he broadcast the sound of his own voice, which was picked up on a receiver a mile away. Stubblefield got a patent—Number 887,357—on May 12, 1908, but owing to his own idiosyncrasies he wouldn't permit knowledge of his invention to be spread about. He wanted a fabulous amount for his creation, and had no takers. He would have been famous—perhaps the father of radio—had he been willing to impart his secret before the patent was granted. But he wasn't.

None of these events had the far-reaching, long-lasting, or revolutionary effect of an experiment conducted by a rather intense young man who had, as a boy, conceived the idea of practical wireless communication.

Guglielmo Marconi had moved to England in 1896, where he took out a patent on a device to transmit sound without wires, and in December of 1901, moved his gear

Preface

to Wales with the idea of transmitting a telegraph code through the air to St. John's, Newfoundland. The dapper Italian electrician settled on sending a single letter of the Morse code—three dots—the letter "S." He felt it would be the most distinguishable sound—a little hard to use in a conversation, but he wasn't ready for a spoken message yet.

Marconi had a good day for his success. Thursday, December 12th, dawned mostly fair, with a crisp and not too strong wind. Today the weather would be called "nearly ideal for transcontinental transmission."

On the coast of Cornwall, Marconi had constructed two high wooden masts with a cable stretched between them to support the antenna. On the Newfoundland side he raised kites and balloons that carried wires through which he hoped to receive the signal.

On the first day, Marconi had receiver trouble, but at noon on the second day he picked up the three dots loud and clear.

Strangely enough, this great broadcasting "first" went unheralded in the nation's press on the day it happened. The New York dailies seemed to ignore it completely, but there was a reason. Marconi was somewhat surreptitious about his actions. The Italian inventor crossed the Atlantic without public announcement to supervise the action on the shores of Newfoundland. Marconi was not averse to publicity, but he felt, unlike many of the American inventors to follow, he would rather have a quiet success on his hands than a well-touted fiasco.

The first press break on the story came on December 16, 1901, in the *Evening Herald* of St. John's, Newfoundland. It was Marconi's own account:

Preface

On arriving in Newfoundland and installing my station on Signal Hill, at the entrance to St. John's, I sent up kites every day this week with the vertical aerial wire appended by which our signals are received. I had previously cabled to my station at Cornwall to begin sending the prearranged signal. On Wednesday my kite blew away, and nothing resulted. Thursday, however, I had better luck. My arrangement was for Cornwall to send at specific intervals between 3 and 6 o'clock P.M. the Morse letter "S," which consists of three dots, thus (. . .). The hours were equivalent to from noon to 3 P.M. at St. John's, and Thursday during these hours myself and my assistant, Mr. Kemp, received these signals under such conditions as assured us they were genuine. We received them through a specially sensitive telephone attached to our instrument, which enables us to detect signals which the instrument would not record.

A social revolution was beginning; and while very few were aware of it, among the scientific-minded, imagination was fired as never before, and homemade wireless receiving sets appeared all over the country.

In 1901 the United States Navy discontinued the use of homing pigeons in favor of wireless telegraphy.

Lee de Forest began wireless experiments at about the same time that Marconi completed his successful transatlantic test. De Forest's first contribution to the soon-to-be industry was a device called "the electrolytic anti-coherer," a new type of wireless detector, which he tried out in Chicago, using a series of barrel hoops connected by wires for an antenna. He was getting a range of from four to five miles.

Briefly, the "coherer" type of receiver was a glass tube filled with metal filings that had to be shaken down each time a signal was received. De Forest's system was a great improvement.

Later, de Forest set up shop in a modest building in Jersey City, New Jersey, as a wireless-set manufacturer under the imposing title of "American Wireless Telegraph Company." A friendly promoter got de Forest an audience in Washington, and he was asked to manufacture sending and receiving sets for the government. He was called upon to equip telegraph stations for the Navy, and in the ensuing years was to give broadcasting some of its most important inventions and developments.

Another American electronic pioneer who figured very heavily in the early progress of broadcasting was Professor Reginald A. Fessenden of the University of Pittsburgh, a former Westinghouse engineer. He had been playing around with wireless telegraphy prior to 1900.

Fessenden and de Forest emerged in the early years of the century as the two Americans who were most generally credited with the development of broadcasting as we know it today.

It was Fessenden who first thought there might be a way of transmitting musical notes and perhaps even the human voice through the air. He developed a detector that was, in reality, a small electric-light bulb that could reproduce music and voice "undulations."

De Forest, shortly afterward in 1906, invented the three-element electron tube. It was called the Audion. This first radio tube revolutionized wireless transmission.

Fessenden, meanwhile, was seeking a machine that would send out "continuous waves" as opposed to the erratic type of "spark and arc" wireless transmission then in use. He believed that if he could develop a smooth and continuous flow of high-frequency vibrations, which couldn't be done with the then popular "spark-gap" system, he might superimpose the human voice on this continuous flow the way Bell had put the human voice on ordinary electric currents. He found his inventor of the machine in Dr. Ernst F. Alexanderson, a brilliant young newcomer to the General Electric plant in Schenectady, New York.

Fessenden began with Alexanderson's machine in 1905 while in the employ of the National Electric Signaling Company. He set up a station at Brant Rock, on the Massachusetts coast. The sending tower was merely a tall metal tube, three feet in diameter, 420 feet high.

There were many false starts. The generator got the belts too hot, and there was much armature trouble. The Alexanderson alternator finally worked, and telegraphic transmission was successfully completed to various ships in the area.

On Christmas Eve, 1906, wireless operators on ships within a radius of a hundred miles of Brant Rock heard the Morse code call, "CQ, CQ." They wondered, at first, if there was a ship in distress. After a few moments the operators on duty could not believe their ears. A human voice was coming out of their earphones! Someone was speaking! It was positively eerie. The talking stopped, and a woman's voice was heard singing. Ships' officers were called in to listen. Next there was the sound of the male voice again, reading a poem. Then came a violin solo. At the end of the performance the male voice asked listeners to write to F. A. Fessenden at Brant Rock, Massachusetts. Scores of the operators responded. This was the first radio "broadcast."

CONTENTS

Contents

xliv

It Sounds Impossible

CHAPTER 1

A Noon in June

Dream maker, you heart breaker,
Wherever you're going
I'm going your way. . . .

T H E rain had stopped, and the late morning sun was forcing its rays between the Seagram Building and the Waldorf Towers. Arthur Godfrey's brown Bentley pulled up in front of the CBS studio building and deposited its famous denizen of the seventh floor at 49 East Fifty-second Street. We nodded hellos as he swung through the doors. John Cooke, the building manager, tapped out his pipe and strolled to the curb to chat with Niel, Godfrey's chauffeur.

Across the street an unfamiliar-looking Pat Suzuki, minus her famous ponytail, her hair shorter—and lighter —walked out of Colbee's Restaurant. She looked skyward inquisitively, then jaywalked to where we stood.

It didn't seem that over five years had passed since she first arrived in town. After a few appearances on the Jack Paar Show she had been signed for *Flower Drum Song*. At that time she was so wary of her ability to read lines that she asked NBC's writers to invent a fictitious character for her which she played under an assumed name on the NBC radio show "Bert Parks' Bandstand."

It Sounds Impossible

The character was that of a frightened little girl singer from Cressy, California, who was looking for her first big break in New York City. The name they gave her was "Susie Schooner." She needn't have worried. She was great —and her singing gave her away immediately. Everybody seemed to know that Susie was Pat.

As she walked through the glass doors and up to the information desk, we noticed that the office girls from WCBS Radio were still taking turns checking the arrival of one of the afternoon's program guests—Rock Hudson. He had been due any minute for the last hour.

Jack Webb, a comparative stranger to New York, was standing on the corner of Fifty-second and Madison, waiting for the light to change. He carried his suitcoat over his arm. Apparently he had just left the main CBS office building at 485. Passersby were doing quick double takes as they recognized him. The light changed, and he headed toward Fifth Avenue.

It was a great day for tourists. For a few minutes it seemed that the woods around Fifty-second Street were full of air celebrities.

We looked across the street at the Columbia Broadcasting System Building. It was beginning to show its age. It had long ago become too small. Even executive personnel were crowded into other buildings in the neighborhood. Some were in the Look Building across the street; others were around the corner at 501. The radio network was housed next to the studio building on Fifty-second. Offices of individual show units were all over town. The TV production center was a mile away on the West Side.

Standing under the aluminum marquee of the studio building, we were waiting for Bob Trout. He was leaving

2

A Noon in June

for Europe in two days, and this would probably be our last chance to catch him before we finished the book. When Trout first came to CBS News, the entire operation consisted of Paul White, the director; a secretary, and Trout. That was it. Millions will never forget that Bob was the voice that announced the end of World War II for Columbia—that his was often the voice that introduced the President of the United States.

The list of friends we had planned to talk to was formidable, but each would contribute a character to the drama, a point of view, a memory.

The dapper six-footer swung into sight. Slim, trim, tailored, Homburg, walking stick, easy gait, dark, moustache—Trout. He was on time, naturally. It was twelve o'clock on the straight up.

We exchanged hellos and then asked him, "Where do you want to eat?"

"I don't care," Trout said. "Someplace around here?"

These were the moments of grave decision. We'd been eating across the street for several weeks, and thought it might be pleasant to change neighborhoods so we wouldn't be hauled into conversations not having to do with the book. If the rain had continued, there wouldn't be a cab in sight. At this minute there were a half-dozen. With the true reaction of conventional New Yorkers, we decided it would be nice to walk. Maybe over to Mike Manuche's.

We walked west, past Cartier's, 21, Toots Shor's and the big excavation on the corner of Sixth Avenue and Fifty-second Street. They had already put up the Plexiglass windows that kept the sidewalk superintendents from falling into the massive pit. Here was to be the new thirty-eight story CBS Building.

It Sounds Impossible

We looked south. A block down was Rockefeller Plaza —the home of NBC. We'd be doing a lot of visiting over there, too. It was a familiar work area for both of us. ABC was a dollar cab ride uptown. There had been so much cross-pollination of talent among the three networks, we knew we'd be in everybody's camp before the book was done.

As we crossed Sixth Avenue and looked toward Broadway, we reminisced a little about the days when network radio helped glamorize midtown—the days when the dance remotes brought them flocking to the hostelries of Times Square. There was Blue Barron's band over at the Green Room of the Hotel Edison. How many years ago? The Three Suns were in the Circus Lounge of the Hotel Picadilly. Sammy Kaye was at the Astor Roof. Glenn Miller introduced "Pennsylvania Six-Five-Thousand" at the Hotel Pennsylvania—across from Penn Station. It's the Statler now.

"Vincent Lopez is still holding forth," Trout remarked.

"And he's still got them lined up for tables at the Taft Grill," we said.

It was almost a shame to leave the bright sun and enter the dim foyer of Manuche's—but once our eyes adjusted we found it cool, pleasant, and plush. The headwaiter found us a table in the back. Trout looked around the room.

"The view from Fifty-second Street," he said. "If the bomb hit this place, two networks would lose half their brass."

After we had ordered, Bob said, "You wanted to get my reaction to V-J Day."

"Yes. You made the announcement."

A Noon in June

"I sure did."

Bob's wife, Kit, had always worked very closely with him, and in those days helped him prepare his news commentaries. She had a complete transcript of everything he said during those exciting hours preceding the end of the big war. After lunch we'd go back to the studio building and tape Trout's story.

The pleasant hour at Manuche's turned into a Can-You-Top-This round robin of stories about radio's early days.

For instance, nobody today would associate Bob Trout with a quiz show, but he was on the very first question-and-answer program—"Professor Quiz." The idea that people could be entertained by listening to somebody ask somebody else an academic question seemed outrageous at first. But, of course, quizzes caught on.

"These were schoolroom questions," Trout said. "A very simple idea. It was a novelty. Then came 'Vox Pop,' and 'Doctor I. Q.,' 'Double or Nothing,' 'Information, Please'—and then it seemed that half the shows on the air were questions and answers."

Bob later emceed another panel-quiz called "Who Said That?"

"Are you going as far back as 'Amos 'n' Andy'?" Trout said.

"Back before KDKA."

"And are you covering some of this so-called entertainment on the air in the last few years?"

"Oh, yes. We're going to call that chapter 'Radio's Worst Hour.'"

"What did you decide was its finest hour?"

"No question," we replied. "World War II—your big

era." We explained that we'd even cover European radio to a degree—with the accent on the BBC.

"Ah, the dear, dear BBC." Bob smiled. "I will never, never forget my first impression of that wonderful facility. I was sent to Britain by CBS, as you know, during the heat of the big war. I was a little apprehensive, as I had every right to be, of living in London when the Germans were dropping those bombs. The lorry ride from the airport to my hotel was one I'll always remember. The shielded headlights of the cars, the eerie half-light on the objects around us. Black was the word for London. A strange mixture, a sense of fear and efficiency, hung in the air. When I got to the hotel room I saw heavy drapes pulled across the windows. I felt that any minute I'd hear the sirens, and then an armada of Junkers dropping a million tons of bombs. Those first few hours in wartime Britain were a bit unsettling, to say the least.

"Over on the night stand," Bob continued, "was a table radio. I was a little too excited to sit down and read a newspaper or a magazine, but I thought that maybe listening to the radio would help. I turned it on and waited for it to warm up, and as I stood in that hotel room, in the middle of the Battle of Britain—waiting for the Blitz, the announcer's voice flooded the room."

Trout grinned. "Here was this wonderfully aloof British voice saying: 'This is the BBC. It is now time for our weekly harmonica lesson.' "

Our lunch date proved rich in material. Trout's story takes its chronological place later in this volume.

As we listened to Bob talk, we thought: Here is the product of a wonderful era. The decades of the miracle of voices through the air. A man who was present and very much accounted for during radio's finest hour.

Trout was part of that golden age, and so were H. V. Kaltenborn and Raymond Gram Swing. There were Ed Murrow and Lowell Thomas, Bill Henry and Eric Sevareid. Bob Hope toured the Army and Navy bases, and Dinah Shore made strong men weep with songs like "You'd Be So Nice to Come Home To." Everybody who had a turntable owned some records by Bing Crosby, Perry Como, and Frank Sinatra. There were Bob Hawk with "Thanks to the Yanks" and Ben Grauer talking to kids whose dads were overseas. And Kate Smith.

But before broadcasting could have a finest hour there had to be thirty years of trial and error to pave the way.

The "stunts" began as early as 1908 when Lee de Forest successfully broadcast from the Eiffel Tower, using a Pathé "talking machine" and playing phonograph records into the Paris air.

In 1910—on a cold January 13th—Enrico Caruso sang into a microphone by special arrangement with the Metropolitan Opera Company. About fifty listeners heard the tenor on receivers at the Park Avenue Library and the Metropolitan Life Insurance building. The praise from the listeners was "lavish." It was Lee de Forest's microphone—and the pioneer had added still another "first" to his impressive string. The New York press was quite unimpressed at first—but as the story of radio unfolded, this single event kept gaining more and more importance as a milestone.

The "reviews" were unmixed. All bad.

From *The New York Times:* "The homeless song waves were kept from finding themselves by constant interruption. Signór Caruso, it was learned later, sang finely at the Opera House (the point of origin) . . . but reporters could only hear a ticking."

The *Sun* bombed the demonstration with: "The guests took turns fitting the receivers over their ears, and one or two of them thought they heard a tenor; they were not positive."

Another news report said, "There was an operator somewhere carrying on a ribald conversation with some other operator, greatly to the detriment of science—and an evening's entertainment."

It was in 1910 that the John Wanamaker stores of Philadelphia and New York began to realize the novelty value of radio as a newspaper space getter and scientific curiosity. They equipped their stores with the most modern and finest equipment available, from the American Marconi Company.

David Sarnoff, at the time, was the enterprising young manager of the Marconi wireless station at Sea Gate, New York. When he learned of the installation of equipment at the Wanamaker stores, he applied for the job of operating the system. This would enable him to keep his evenings free for further study in electronics at Pratt Institute.

It was young Sarnoff who, while sitting at his instrument panel at Wanamaker's store in New York, in April of 1912, picked up the tragic news of the *Titanic* disaster.

The first message he received through the air was, "The S.S. *Titanic* ran into iceberg. Sinking fast."

The birth of radio news.

It was Sarnoff, too, who carried on the first experiments

in transmitting music from the Wanamaker store on a regularly scheduled basis.

In 1916 the man who was to become Chairman of the Board of the Radio Corporation of America issued a paper that became a favorite of broadcast historians. Today we'd call it a long memo. It was directed by Sarnoff to Edward J. McNally, who was then the general manager of the Marconi Company.

It read, in part:

I have in mind a plan of development which would make radio a "household utility" in the same sense as the piano or phonograph. The idea is to bring music into the house by wireless.

While this has been tried in the past by wires, it has been a failure because wires do not lend themselves to this scheme. . . .

The receiver can be designed in the form of a simple "Radio Music Box" and arranged for several different wave lengths, which should be changeable with the throwing of a single switch or pressing of a single button. . . .

The Radio Music Box can be supplied with amplifying tubes and a loudspeaking telephone, all of which can be neatly mounted in one box. The box can be placed on a table in the parlor or living room. . . .

Baseball scores can be transmitted in the air by the use of one set being installed at the Polo Grounds. . . .

This proposition would be especially interesting to farmers and others living in outlying districts removed from the cities. By the purchase of a "Radio Music Box" they could enjoy concerts, lectures, music, recitals, etc., which may be going on in the nearest city within their radius. . . .

The manufacture of the "Radio Music Box" . . . in large

9

quantities would make possible their sale at a moderate figure of perhaps $75.00 per outfit. . . .

From the time of the inception of his scheme for producing "Radio Music Boxes" to the actual manufacture of the device, four years had elapsed and much had happened within the American Marconi Company.

In 1917, at the outset of America's entry into the First World War, the government took over all wireless stations, including Marconi's.

The General Electric Company had offered to purchase the Marconi Company interests, and after complicated negotiations that had international overtones, and after a tremendous battle against government ownership of wireless communications, G.E. and the Marconi Company were ready to launch the Radio Corporation of America in 1919.

By the fall of that year, after RCA had taken over the affairs of the American Marconi Company, David Sarnoff was made general manager of the new corporation. Edward McNally was its president. Sarnoff still had great faith in his Music Box idea, and resubmitted it, along with a financial prognosis, to E. W. Rice, Jr., president of General Electric. Though he admitted there was still much experimentation to be done in developing the device, he estimated that it would be reasonable to expect sales of one million boxes within a period of three years. Still suggesting a price of $75 per unit, he guessed at gross sales of 75 million if they moved 100,000 of them the first year, 300,000 the second year, and 600,000 the third. His guess was slightly low, which would indicate how well Sarnoff knew his market potential.

In 1922 the first "Radio Music Box" came off the assembly line. In the radio boom, consumers gobbled up $11,000,000 worth in the first year. Sarnoff's educated guess for the second year was on the nose, with gross sales amounting to $22,500,000. The public paid $50,000,000 for radios the next year, for a three-year total of $83,-500,000.

The rush was on. The industry was alive. America had given birth to an adult.

CHAPTER 2

Something
for Nothing

S K I R T S were going up "far beyond any modest limitation." The hemlines were a shocking nine inches above
the ground. Nice girls started smoking cigarettes. Some
said the songs of the day suggested immorality—"Three
o'Clock in the Morning," "I Wish I Could Shimmy Like
My Sister Kate."

The nation went dry with the prohibition of liquor,
and along with the Eighteenth Amendment came the hip
flask and bathtub gin.

Another Amendment—the Nineteenth—gave women
the right to vote, but it was to take a few years before they
really started to get into politics.

The year 1920 was one for the beginnings of great projects. The Panama Canal was declared formally completed,
the League of Nations held its first meeting in London,
the dial telephone system was introduced, and John L.

Something for Nothing

Lewis was elected president of the United Mine Workers Union.

Big corporations, realizing the possibilities of radio, were beginning to underwrite broadcasting stations. Amateur broadcasters were disappearing.

But for the most part, early radio receivers were home-made creations—a coil of wire wrapped around an oatmeal box and a "cat's whisker"—a thin tungsten wire that touched a tiny pile of silica. You could pick up a "crystal detector" at almost any hardware store very cheaply. Of course you wouldn't buy a whole store-made crystal set. It wasn't smart. You wired up your own. You needed some Number 20 wire, a couple of contact clips, a few strips of copper, a sheet of sandpaper, pliers and a screwdriver, and you were in business.

It was rumored that radio "bugs" got so nutty that they'd run to the store, buy a box of Quaker Oats and dump out the cereal just to get the box to make another darn-fool crystal set.

In 1920 the nation was in a state of general prosperity, with food prices soaring. A new phrase crept into Americans' conversation—"the high cost of living."

The motion-picture industry was making itself felt with flickers that had both stars and stories, and Will Rogers made his film debut in *Jes' Call Me Bill*.

The population of the country topped the 100 million mark.

It was to be a year of social progress and change. A daring young housewife might appear on the streets in bobbed hair, wearing a bit of rouge. Her young husband was an admirer of—or probably even drove—an open touring car with detachable side curtains. If they had a little money, there might be a phonograph in their home or apartment. If they were fairly well off, it would be the mahogany floor model. If they were loaded, comparatively, they would entertain their guests with music from their newly acquired player piano, and if the husband was a scientific nut, they owned a cat's-whisker crystal set with double-ear headset, because by Thanksgiving there were sounds in the air.

WBAY and WEAF in New York were broadcasting programs of a sort on a highly tentative basis, the latter carrying the description of a football game on October 28th from Stagg Field in Chicago where Princeton was drubbing the University of Chicago. New Yorkers were enjoying as much as three hours of radio entertainment a day—on a good day.

KDKA, in Pittsburgh, scheduled its first broadcast on November 2, 1920. The construction of the station was accomplished by the late Dr. Frank Conrad, then assistant chief engineer of the Westinghouse Company. His assistant was a radio "ham" from Kalamazoo, Michigan, by the name of D. G. Little—who subsequently rose to be assistant manager and consulting engineer in Westinghouse Electronics division. As well he should. Conrad and Little did the lion's share of inventive and creative broadcasting in the early 1920's which gave the industry some pretty sensational press. At the outset KDKA was the leader in early program ideas and concepts. The station broadcast the first regularly scheduled church broadcast and provided the necessary remote pickup. The latter part of this "first" was really a necessity because KDKA did not have formal broadcast studios that would accommodate such a program for the first six months of its existence. KDKA

14

operated from a tent. They came up with the first market reports for farmers and the first barn dance.

The sensation of the year in radio in 1920 was KDKA's broadcasting of the Harding-Cox presidential election returns on November 2nd. The event was local, but the nation's press picked it up with fervor. They knew about wireless, but this was a stroke of programming genius.

Arrangements were made by Dr. Conrad with the Pittsburgh *Post* to secure election returns by telephone. To increase the audience of KDKA that day, the engineering department installed loudspeakers in the ballroom of the Edgewood Club, a suburban Pittsburgh community center where many citizens gathered—including, on this night, a goodly number of Westinghouse folks.

The broadcast originated in a tiny makeshift shack atop one of the Westinghouse manufacturing buildings in East Pittsburgh. There was no "studio." A single room accommodated the transmitting equipment, turntable for records, and a six-man broadcasting crew.

KDKA went on the air at 6:00 P.M. and continued until noon the following day, issuing returns separated by phonograph music. News of Cox's concession and Harding's victory via radio was exciting fare—particularly when the few crystal-set owners of the day noted the downpour of rain on election night and smiled contentedly, in their warm homes, while the usual crowds stood drenched in front of outdoor bulletin boards.

The gang at the Edgewood Club whooped it up and kept calling the station to ask for more news and less music.

A ship off the coast of Virginia, carrying American troops from Puerto Rico to New York, picked up the re-

15

turns. The excited radioman, hearing the broadcast on his earphone, hastened to deliver the returns to his captain, expecting them to be posted on the ship's bulletin board. But the skipper, who had once been the victim of an early-day radio "hoax," was dubious, and would not permit the bulletins to be posted.

But the crystal-set owners were convinced, the international publicity was laudatory, and radio stampeded ahead.

By August 1st of 1921, there were only two new stations on the air, but this figure jumped to 11 by September 1st, and by the close of 1921 there were over 30 stations on the air.

In 1922, transmitter towers popped up like dandelions in the spring. Radio had come to Seattle, Los Angeles, Portland, Denver, Chicago, New Orleans, Minneapolis, and most every major market. By the end of 1922 over 200 stations were broadcasting programs, and this "passing novelty" had an audience of over 3,000,000 radio homes. The receivers cost their owners from $50 to $100 each.

"Wireless concerts" were the rage, and that year found Westinghouse maintaining four "canned concert" stations.

A unique item of local news cropped up in daily papers all over the country. Hardly a day went by that some local citizen didn't fall off his roof while installing a radio antenna.

In Kansas City the idea was to see if you could "get" WGY in Schenectady. The folks in Minneapolis would stay up half the night to see if they could receive a signal from KDKA in Pittsburgh, and the minute the call letters were identifiable they would immediately switch to see if they could "get" WBAP in Fort Worth. The greatest boon to ardent radio fans of the day was the discovery that the ordinary bedspring made a very acceptable and effective aerial.

Another unique ramification that radio brought to the manners and mores of Americans was the constantly increasing numbers of people sitting with earphones on, staring into space, transfixed and glassy-eyed, whose only comment if someone entered the room was "Sh-hh-hh!"

With this kind of ready market, it was natural that the nation should suddenly see a blossoming forth of all sorts of radio manuals and listening guides. For the most part they were quite unimaginative, and carried a semi-correct list of programs for any of the stations in the nation who had some vague idea of what they were going to put on the air.

In the first issue of *Radio Broadcast,* in May of 1922, the editor said that the rate of increase in the number of people who spent at least part of the evening listening "is almost in-comprehensible." The magazine pointed out that anyone who had tried to buy a radio in a store often found himself in the fourth or fifth row, waiting his turn, only to be told, when he finally reached the counter, that he could place an order but that the store was sold out.

The magazine predicted—firmly—that "before the radio movement has reached its height and before the market for receiving apparatus becomes saturated there will be at least five million receiver sets in the United States."

The prediction was a little shy. At this writing manufacturers are turning out over ten million radio sets and over five million TV sets a *year.* There are 183 million radio receivers in over 98 percent of American households, and an additional 47 million sets in cars.

It Sounds Impossible

The first KDKA broadcasts had great novelty impact in the Pittsburgh area, and occasional receiver sets from other parts of the nation could get a sporadic signal from Dr. Conrad's sending apparatus, but the idea was actually slow in spreading at first. There were technical difficulties in transmitting a usable signal, and radio sets were, for the most part, still quite inefficient.

Interest, of course, increased in direct ratio with the number of radio stations coming on the air. The Detroit *News* launched station WWJ shortly after KDKA's early sounds. In 1920 Westinghouse planned its second station —WJZ, Newark, New Jersey—later to become WABC, New York. (And WABC, New York, became WCBS, New York; and WEAF became WNBC, which became WRCA, which again became WNBC. While the Bible has its "begats," the history of radio is studded with "becames.")

As was later to be the case with television, the 1920's saw a formidable string of radio "firsts." Everybody who turned around in broadcasting was doing something for the first time. Among the more important firsts—important in that it began a pattern in the industry—was the broadcast of the first radio commercial.

The American Telephone and Telegraph Company established radio station WEAF on August 16, 1922, and twelve days later broadcast the first "spot" announcement. Well, maybe "spot" isn't the word. It was more like a ten-minute filibuster on behalf of the Queensborough Corporation of Jackson Heights, New York. The time: 5:15 P.M. An august voice was picked up on crystal sets saying:

ANNOUNCER: This afternoon the radio audience is to be addressed by Mr. Blackwell of the Queensborough Corporation who, through arrangements made by the Griffen Radio

Something for Nothing

Service, will say a few words concerning Nathaniel Hawthorne and the desirability of fostering the helpful community spirit and the healthful, unconfined home life that were Hawthorne ideals. Ladies and gentlemen, Mr. Blackwell.

BLACKWELL: It is fifty-eight years since Nathaniel Hawthorne, the greatest of American fictionists, passed away. To honor his memory the Queensborough Corporation, creator and operator of the tenant-owned system of apartment houses at Jackson Heights, New York City, has named its latest group of high-grade dwellings "Hawthorne Court."

I wish to thank those within the sound of my voice for the opportunity afforded me to urge this vast radio audience to seek the recreation of God's great outdoors! There should be more Hawthorne sermons preached about the inadequacy and general hopelessness of the congested city home. . . . Apartments in congested cities are *failures* . . . but imagine a congested city apartment lifted bodily to the middle of a large garden within twenty minutes' travel of the city's business center. . . . Dr. Royal S. Copeland, Health Commissioner of New York, recently declared that any person who preached leaving the crowded city for the open country was a public-spirited citizen and a benefactor to the race. Shall we not follow this advice and become the benefactors he praises? Let us resolve . . .

And so it went. On and on.

There is no record of sales results following this first advertisement, but in retrospect, Mr. Blackwell didn't do badly, copywise. There are still vestiges of this type of thing on some stations today. Some set to music.

Although radio began to grow in terms of audience, in the early twenties, it was an economic bomb. It had no acceptance as an advertising medium. Despite the fact that magazine circulation was off 30 percent because, experts said, of radio, and even though the little black box had knocked the record business downstairs with disc sales falling off 85 to 90 percent, the medium was financially chaste. Station owners were discovering that it cost money to operate, and there didn't seem to be any of the green stuff around. Established advertisers used newspapers, handbills, window displays, and billboards.

Confounding the issue were the actors and actresses of Broadway and Hollywood who were making noises like they wanted money to perform on the air. The American Society of Composers, Authors, and Publishers was becoming a little testy about radio stations playing recorded music over the air without payment. Then, too, radio had a big electric bill, salaries for announcers, engineers, and secretarial help, and general operating expenses.

Advertising, at first, didn't seem to be a practical answer to broadcasting's money problems. At a time when only a dozen or so of the hundreds of stations in operation were breaking even, Secretary Hoover helped not at all when he announced:

"The American people will never stand for advertising on the radio!"

This was the Big Poser in an industry where everybody seemed to be making a buck except the man who put the entertainment on the air. There were suggestions that a subscription system might work whereby a lecturer could realize payment by mail from the people who heard him speak by radio. There was speculation that perhaps a number of "public-spirited citizens" could be rounded up who would contribute directly to the support of stations in their own localities. After all, do they not endow libraries,

Something for Nothing

athletic fields, and museums? Someone else suggested that radio be financed by the public contributing to a common fund which would be controlled by an elected board. Still others thought radio should be subsidized by the government. This was to become a particularly tender point a bit later when the government stepped into broadcasting with firm controls on station allocations. Some manufacturers considered coin-operated radio boxes, but the fact was that people were getting something for nothing and it was too late to change it.

So it was radio's cry that stations could not pay artists money because there was none. Early entertainers worked radio shows for the "publicity."

Adding to the new industry's frustrations were the whispering "campaigns"—probably started out of simple fear and ignorance.

Stories were circulated freely that radio listening was actually bad for the ears and that a radio set in the house was a peril. Gossip had it that electrical storms started fires in homes with radios. Others imagined that the waves sent out by transmitters could be injurious. The outbreak of many diseases were often blamed on "the waves in the house."

Station WHAS in Louisville had gripe letters as early as 1922, a couple of which went something like this:

"My little girl throwed up in school today. She ain't given to throwin up and they say its the radio and you got to give her sumthing."

A southern gentleman dressed in the frock coat of the backwoods pastor-farmer descended on WHAS demanding that broadcasting be curbed. He said that he had taken a walk across his farm when a flock of blackbirds passed over.

It Sounds Impossible

Suddenly, one of them fell to the ground, dead. "Your radio waves must have struck it," he shouted. "Suppose that wave would have struck me! Well!"

Another woman of the 1920's wrote that she couldn't sleep at night. Someone had told her that the broadcasting waves played over the metal springs in her mattress, and she was afraid to get into bed. She had sat up for forty-eight hours. The woman asked the station to stop it or she would have to sue.

As if this weren't bad enough, there was a bit of religious agitation making the rounds about radio. With theater personalities coming into the medium, there suddenly grew overtones of "worldliness" which some faiths were continually putting down. Many preachers were dead set against religious-minded individuals having what amounted to a "showplace" in their living rooms. However, the religious prejudice was short-lived as hundreds and then thousands of pastors found the radio an instrument of inspiration and, incidentally, a great source of revenue for them.

"Remember us in your prayers, and keep those letters comin', friends!"

The Stars Appear

V I N C E N T   L O P E Z has a very corny orchestra. It is so corny that anyone can dance to its music. It is so square that couples line up ten deep at the door of the Taft Grill to wait for tables. Lopez is so "Mickey Mouse" that he is one of the very few who is still making a bundle in the band business.

Lopez was the first big-name bandleader to broadcast on radio on any kind of regular basis. Lopez was the father of the dance remote.

The Vincent Lopez who sat across the table from us at the Taft only resembled the Vincent Lopez of 1921. Long gone is the slicked-back pompadour parted in the middle. Today he wears a crew cut. In his days at the Hotel Pennsylvania and the St. Regis, Lopez wouldn't be caught dead conducting without tails. Today he wears a simply designed tux and black tie when he leads the band.

"What decided you on the crew cut?" we asked him.

"Somebody told me that with my hair parted in the middle and the tails I looked like a penguin," he replied.

"But in the twenties, looking like a penguin was a very big deal."

We asked Vincent if he remembered that first broadcast.

"I'll never forget it," he said. "It was pretty funny in retrospect—considering how simple things are now. And, I guess it was a little frightening in a way, too. I did it as a favor for Tommy Cowan."

Tom Cowan had been taken from one of the factory departments at Westinghouse in New Jersey and made WJZ's first announcer. He also arranged programs and acted as a utility infielder for the new station. The "impresario" of WJZ was a man named Dr. William H. Easton. Easton had great faith in Cowan's inventiveness— and encouraged him to promote exciting radio fare.

"Just about everything Tommy did was a 'first,'" Vincent said. "The guy absolutely fascinated me with his talk about radio. To hear Tommy talk about waves through the air was to be awed.

"I was playing at the Pennsylvania Grill back in November of 1921 when Tommy walked in looking like he had been stabbed in the back by his best friend. I left the bandstand and sat with him at his table. He told me he had a great idea—bringing an entire Broadway show over to the WJZ studios in Newark and broadcasting the whole thing on the air."

"This made him sad?"

"No. The idea was great. But he ran into some trouble getting it on the air. Tommy had made a deal with Carl Helm, who was then the press agent for a pithy—but somewhat naughty—Broadway show called *Tangerine*. He was supposed to bring the entire cast to Jersey on a Sunday night when the theater was dark. It was the biggest entertainment idea yet in radio."

The year 1921 had been a big one on Broadway. Al Jolson was starring in *Bombo,* Lynn Fontanne was in *Dulcy,* and Frank Crummit and Julia Sanderson were hits in *Tangerine.* Both Crummit and Miss Sanderson were to find fame in radio—but not in November of 1921 on WJZ.

"What happened to Cowan's plan?"

"A few bluenoses and clergymen who read about the show started screaming objections. They considered radio akin to show business—and therefore evil. A menace to morals. They called *Tangerine* salacious. They said, too, that putting a Broadway show on radio on a Sunday night would cause people to stay home from church. And, anyway, nobody had the right to broadcast on the Lord's day."

"And Westinghouse demurred?"

"They wouldn't touch it. It was a Saturday when Tommy came into the Pennsylvania Grill. I asked him when the broadcast was supposed to happen, and he told me it was the next night," Lopez continued.

"I told him: 'Look, we don't work tomorrow night. Why don't I take the band over there in place of *Tangerine?*'

"I'll never forget the way Tommy's face lit up," Lopez said.

We've seen that scene in a dozen grade-B movies since. But Lopez and Cowan were the first to play it—live.

Lopez's offer to have his band replace the Broadway show was more magnanimous in 1921 than it would be today. Newark was not as accessible to New York City. Traffic jams and distance dampened the ardor of many artists who were based in Gotham.

It Sounds Impossible

"Tommy went out and rented a big Pierce-Arrow to get the boys over there," Lopez continued, "but I canceled it. I told him I thought the Jersey tubes would be quicker and easier—and anyway the whole band wouldn't fit into a touring car. Cowan thought that this was too, too simple, and somehow unshowmanlike. But he arranged to have a fleet of cabs at the Jersey end of the tubes."

Lopez had never been in a radio station before and didn't know what to expect. WJZ's studio was a converted cloakroom in the Westinghouse factory building. The coats were jammed together a bit and a space about 10 feet by 18 feet was made available. The transmitting equipment was installed in a shack on the roof with a line running down to the studio.

"I remember we had to walk up a rickety stairway to the studio. It was hardly big enough for a man walking sideways, let alone a band carrying drums and horns and fiddles. I wondered what kind of a cheap outfit this was. Naturally, I didn't find a grand piano. It was an old upright. And upright it was . . . just barely.

"Cowan had built himself some acoustical devices based on experience in recording. The room was hung with "absorbent" drapes. Cowan had dyed them a ghastly red. Uniformity, I guess. Heavy rugs on the floor helped deaden the studio sound. This was all very good, but it got so hot in there that during any warm day they had to prop open the door to keep the talent from dying. Of course, that let all the sounds of Newark in.

"Anyway, I'll never forget that microphone. Like everything else, it, too, was an experiment. I had the brasses work across the mike, not directly into it. I still broadcast that way. It must have been quite a picture.

26

The Stars Appear

Musicians all dressed up—shiny brass horns, drums, music stands—all jammed into a cloakroom, everybody a little nervous.

"Cowan was happy as a lark. We were just about to go on the air when he remembered something. What's the program? We were suddenly on the air, and Cowan turned to me and said, 'Mr. Lopez will announce tonight's program of music!' I died. I shook my head no. He shook his head yes. So I stepped up to this ugly thing called a microphone, and said, 'Hello everybody! Lopez speaking!' "

But that's all Lopez said. Cowan jumped to his side and asked, "Is that all you're going to say, Mr. Lopez?"

"That's enough for me," Lopez said.

So it was Cowan who ad-libbed his way through Lopez's first radio concert. Among other things, the Lopez band played "Anitra's Dance," "Celeste Aïda," and Vincent did "Canadian Capers" as a piano solo.

As soon as Lopez was off the air, the telephone started to ring. Most of the calls were from Westinghouse officials who were not only pleased but surprised that Cowan had managed to replace the theatrical production so satisfactorily.

November 27, 1921. A ninety-minute music show. The first "live" broadcast by a famous dance orchestra.

At that time there was no thought of a remote-control dance-music broadcast, but Lopez quickly recognized the publicity value of radio generally, and suggested to Cowan that it might be a good idea if the band again broadcast from Newark but, this time, to augment the radio audience by putting a great big receiver in the Grill Room of the Hotel Pennsylvania. Radio was still such a novelty he figured it might give the customers quite a thrill. They could dance to the music of their favorite orchestra in New York while the boys made music in Jersey.

Lopez recalls the engineers setting the contraption up in the Grill.

"It looked like a cross between a foghorn and a guillotine."

Lopez's boss, E. M. Statler, the famous hotel magnate, thought the stunt had some merit, and advertised it quite widely. A large crowd showed up.

"Of course, I couldn't know what was going on in the Grill while I was in Newark," Lopez said. "We broadcast a specially prepared program of easy-to-dance-to music. Then we rushed back to the hotel to find out how it had been received and what kind of impression it had made on the customers."

Lopez smiled. If the recollection was painful, he didn't show it.

"Everybody greeted us with open arms. At last they could *dance*. All that had come out of the big machine were grunts and groans and a strange crackling noise that the engineers kept referring to as 'static.'

"Well—we got our names in the paper, anyway."

Cowan and Lopez became close friends. The bandleader had found a real champion in the announcer from WJZ. Cowan wanted Lopez to become a regular WJZ feature, and Vincent opened still another door in radio. He asked Cowan if there was any way to put a microphone right on the bandstand at the Pennsylvania Grill and send the music down wires—or something—to the station in Newark.

"The telephone company says it isn't feasible," Cowan answered. He had thought of the same thing earlier. "But let me see if Western Union can work something out."

The Stars Appear

Western Union came through with an installation after about a month of study, and on the Thursday just before Christmas in 1921, Vincent Lopez did the first remote dance-band pickup.

He "plugged" the event in advance on WJZ, inviting listeners to come to the Grill and witness an *actual broadcast*.

The response was immediate. Within an hour after his first "promo" on the air, every table in the Pennsylvania Grill had been reserved by phone, and there was a waiting list. On the night of the broadcast, Seventh Avenue from Thirty-third to Thirty-fourth streets looked a little like New Year's eve in Times Square. The entire hotel was sold out by midafternoon.

"I *really* realized there were people out there," Lopez said, "when I made the mistake of offering a photograph of myself to anyone who would write in. The next day's mail filled ten big clothes hampers. I just couldn't take care of it. I apologized on the air, and changed the offer to say that anyone telephoning the Hotel Pennsylvania would get a picture. The incoming calls actually knocked out one of the mid-Manhattan telephone exchanges, and of course flooded the hotel's switchboards.

"Statler got complaints from people who were trying to get room reservations and finally gave up because of the busy signal. He told me to get my own switchboard the next time. But he thought radio had some definite possibilities."

In those days Lopez was in hot competition for popularity with Paul Whiteman who, by 1921, was already wearing the mantle of "The King of Jazz." Lopez's attitude toward radio and his eagerness to enter the field didn't hurt him a bit. Whiteman was to be a holdout for another year. The King dismissed the new medium with the comment that radio was for kids who liked to build crystal sets and fool around with them, but Lopez felt that this growing thing would create new fans for him. He was right.

His famous "Hello, everybody! Lopez speaking!" is still his radio trademark as he broadcasts from the Taft Grill in Times Square over forty years later.

Tom Cowan did succeed in bringing a Broadway Show to radio. The *Tangerine* incident served only to inspire him. The production he chose was *The Perfect Fool* with Ed Wynn, a hit that had been enjoying a long run at the George M. Cohan Theatre. Again, Cowan proposed that the entire troup be brought to WJZ's studios in Newark.

Ed Wynn wasn't exactly in love with the medium at first. He was extremely wary of the microphone, and approached it gingerly. Performers were all very suspicious of the microphone, and Wynn was more than somewhat so. He used some of his best material in front of the contraption. After each gag he would stare it down. He knew nothing would be coming back, but it unnerved him to be telling stories to a tin can.

Dripping with perspiration after four or five of his best jokes, he finally turned to the studio announcer and said, "I can't do anything!"

The announcer nodded but motioned for Ed to continue. As "The Perfect Fool" struggled along, the announcer quickly recruited all the humanity in the area—electricians, cleaning women, telephone operators, and performers whose turn was yet to come. Anybody who was standing around was gently pushed into the Wynn studio.

The Stars Appear

With an audience responding to his material, Wynn came alive. He couldn't envision listeners at home individually convulsed, but a live audience! This was for showfolk!

So Ed Wynn was the father of the studio audience.

"Mike fright" was to become the big topic of discussion among show-business personalities who took a swing at radio. More than one top star was quoted as "feeling funny" while on the air. At NBC today is a collection of historical microphones, the most ornate of which is called "The Mary Pickford Mike." It looks like a lamp. It was built that way to camouflage the microphone during Miss Pickford's radio debut. The carbon apparatus was hidden by an apricot-colored cloth shade. It would frighten today's performer half to death.

With stars of the magnitude of Wynn and Pickford on the air, even sporadically, radio became a very real economic threat to other forms of entertainment. Theater owners, motion-picture exhibitors, carnival operators, anybody who vied for a paid audience, felt very uneasy about the new competitor. Enough of the big names of the stage and screen were drifting into radio by 1924 to cause *Variety,* the show-business monitor and philosopher, to say:

"Radio is the biggest thing the amusement business ever had to encounter as opposition. Show business is helpless against it."

CHAPTER 4

The Government
Gets into the Act

B E F O R E radio became an entertainment medium it was simply referred to as "wireless transmission," and belonged primarily to the military. Because this means of communication showed great promise during World War I as a combat facility, it was quite natural that it should come under some sort of government control.

The United States Department of Commerce found itself with wireless communications under its wing in August of 1912. At that time radio was used mostly for ship-to-shore communications, and was a handy thing to have. No one foresaw its commercial possibilities. There was a vaguely written law that required licensing of operators, but nothing covered "general" broadcasting.

When Herbert Hoover became Secretary of Commerce during Harding's administration in 1921, there was still no precedence about licensing or not licensing radio sta-

The Government Gets into the Act

tions. Hoover saw that it was possible for the station situation to become chaotic in view of the fact that when he took office there were less than 50,000 receiving sets in the country and that within six months the count had jumped to a million. Where once there had been two stations there were suddenly over three hundred.

There was no real problem of conflict of frequencies at first. Because most of the stations were built by amateurs, and operated on very low power, their wavelengths didn't overlap or interfere. But as the stations increased power, the trouble began.

The prime prerequisite for operating a station was the ability to send a signal into the air. Grab a spot on the dial and let 'er rip.

Station owners on good frequencies found themselves drowned out by other operators on similar frequencies that caused their programs to slosh over into the other station's backyard. Getting two or more programs at once on the same dial position was quite common in the 1920's.

The industry itself was anxious for regulation. Something had to be done about policing the wavelengths and assigning them, and the job fell to Herbert Hoover, then Secretary of Commerce.

In February of 1922, he called a conference of all branches of the radio industry—the broadcasters, set manufacturers, amateurs, and government agencies interested in wireless communication. Hoover's address to the conference marked the beginning of what we know today as the Federal Communications Commission.

In his speech he pointed out that the nation had witnessed in the last four or five months "one of the most astonishing things that has come under my observation in American life. The department [of Commerce] estimates today that there are over six hundred thousand persons— one estimate being a million—who possess wireless telephone receiving sets whereas there were less than fifty thousand of them a year ago.

"The comparative cheapness of receiving sets bids fair to make them almost universal in the American home."

The use of radio for communications "between single individuals," as in the case of the telephone, was "perfectly hopeless," he said.

"Obviously, if ten million telephone subscribers are crying through the air for their mates, they'll never make a junction. So wireless telephone between individuals must be suppressed, or limited to very narrow use.

"We who are here," Hoover said, "are primarily interested in broadcasting. It becomes a primary public interest to say who is to do the broadcasting and under what circumstances and with what type of material. It is inconceivable that we should allow so great a possibility for service and for news, for entertainment and education and for vital commercial purposes to be drowned in advertising chatter!

"There is . . . the necessity to establish public right over the radio bands. There must be no national regret that we have parted with so great a national asset."

Setting up a good police system over the airwaves presented many problems. The industry suffered growing pains, and conflicts arose that needed talking out. It wasn't clearly established just how this whole broadcasting business would resolve itself, and who would own what on what terms.

The Government Gets into the Act

Hoover noted the beginnings of broadcasting in Britain with great interest. Despite his dislike for commercials on the air, he didn't approve of England's governmental broadcast monopoly. He went on record as saying that he believed that free speech and general communications would be safer in private hands.

A voluntary system of control of the airways was set up in which the stations who were assigned frequencies agreed to confine their signals to these wavelengths and not move around on the dial.

Hoover then urged the passage of legislation in Congress that would make the control system an enforceable law. The voluntary system, however, was such a success that Congress delayed the bill—and in 1925 it died between the House and the Senate.

In 1927 a few stations began breaking away from the voluntary control system, going so far as to pirate the wavelength on which another station was operating. Trouble began as one Chicago broadcaster grabbed another station's frequency and went to court to test the strength of the Radio Act in controlling wavelengths.

Congress finally woke up, and the Federal Radio Commission was formed—the predecessor of the Federal Communications Commission. President Coolidge appointed five members to arbitrate radio's difficulties and to reallocate the positions of the stations on the air.

By the time the FRC was formed, there were more than a thousand stations. This number was reduced to 708 in November of 1927.

Hoover still had his problems. There were a few scofflaws around the country who persisted in broadcasting all over the dial.

It Sounds Impossible

In Los Angeles there was Aimee Semple McPherson, a lady evangelist who, in 1927, made Billy Sunday look like a piker behind the pulpit. She served up fire, brimstone, saints and sinners in gross lots, and claimed Sunday "gate receipts" of up to $10,000 for a single "performance." Her Temple was a great tourist attraction—and many visitors stayed to pray and pay. On the side she sold cemetery lots and built a radio station.

It came to the attention of the Federal Government that Aimee Semple was not strictly observing the Radio Commission's regulations about staying in one spot on the dial. She was all over everybody's wavelength, undoubtedly figuring it was the Lord's air and she had every right in the world to it as a promoter of the Lord.

Hoover had warned Miss McPherson several times about sticking to her frequency, and finally sent an FRC inspector to the West Coast to close her station.

Aimee Semple wired to Hoover: ORDER YOUR MINIONS OF SATAN TO LEAVE MY STATION ALONE. YOU CANNOT EXPECT THE ALMIGHTY TO ABIDE BY YOUR WAVELENGTH NONSENSE. WHEN I OFFER MY PRAYERS TO HIM I MUST FIT IN WITH HIS WAVE RECEPTION. OPEN THIS STATION AT ONCE.

Hoover convinced her that if she hired a proper manager and stayed on the allocated frequency she could have her license back.

Hoover was afraid he was facing the inevitable when he looked around for ways in which radio stations could support themselves financially, and still keep radio free from total government control. Advertising seemed to be the only answer, and he issued a suggestion that he later realized was a hopeless idea.

The Government Gets into the Act

The "Hoover Method" of broadcast advertising was for the sponsor to announce briefly at the beginning of the program that he was providing the following entertainment as a public service. This announcement would be repeated at the end of the program—omitting any advertising during the show. Hoover felt that if an advertiser limited himself to a simple statement as to the nature of his business and the type of goods he had for sale, people would respond out of sheer respect and delight. Hoover also believed that the very idea of not being annoyed with repetitious claims and counterclaims would appeal to the good nature of the American consumer.

Hoover once said that he often felt, when listening to a latter-day commercial on the air, that he would never buy that product. The noisy approach and the "hard sell" offended him.

Mr. Hoover had a point, however—a point politicians might heed when planning election campaign strategy on radio and television today. They have gone Madison Avenue in a big way since.

Over the years, the problems of the Federal Communications Commission have multiplied—partially because of the Commission itself. It now has jurisdiction over some 3,500 standard broadcast stations and nearly a thousand FM operations.

Where Mr. Hoover was troubled about advertising on the air, the present Commission considers this aspect only one of its many concerns. Today's FCC worries about equal time for political candidates, good taste in programming, promotional contests conducted by stations to build audience, the integrity of station management, the news policy of a station, how station records are kept, and whether a station is truly offering a community service. The FCC has since become so powerful an agency that keeping a station on its frequency is the very least of its functions. Stations who do not toe the line face license suspension, or at least a stiff fine.

If It Moves . . .
Broadcast It

O N C E the microphone got outside there was no keeping it in. Anyplace in the world became a radio studio. It was a great challenge to broadcasting's ingenuity and resourcefulness.

Wires were stretched to churches, sport arenas, theaters, hotels, nightclubs, circus grounds, parades, and prisons. Broadcasts came from moving planes, ships at sea, and balloons. Anyplace—the more unlikely, the better.

And they called them Special Events.

Even some of the most ridiculous special events, however, made signal contributions to the growth and development of radio. The novelty of wireless sound mixed with showmanship made news at every turn. Radio became the talk of the day in newspapers.

The early years spewed up a wild assortment of screwball antics. The race for "firsts" in coverage was highly competitive, often idiotic, and, naturally, the public ate it up. It was a lot of fun.

"Hey, Charlie," a citizen of the twenties might say, "did you happen to hear over the radio they were fryin' an egg on the sidewalk right downtown?"

Or, "I guess we don't have to go to church anymore. We can just tune it in over the radio!"

After a while it became quite evident that the listener was not so amused or amazed at these programs as were the men who dreamed them up. Slowly, broadcasters began to realize that program content was far more important than wild ideas or improbable remote points.

In looking back over those broadcasting milestones, the number of "firsts" is overwhelming. Anybody who put a microphone anyplace in those days was creating or committing a "first." There are probably more "firsts" in broadcasting than in any other industry. Every station in the nation has its own first somethings.

In 1921, KDKA, Pittsburgh, broadcast direct from a theater. The same station did the first outdoor pickup of record.

In 1922, KHJ, Los Angeles, broadcast an Easter service which was picked up on the steamship *Yale* and "magnivoxed" to an assembly of passengers bound for San Francisco. Film star Douglas Fairbanks became a reporter for KHJ and did daily reports from the '22 Rotary International convention.

On June 14th of that year, WEAR, Baltimore, presented the first American President on radio. Warren G. Harding broadcast the dedication of the Francis Scott Key monument at Fort McHenry.

In 1923, WGY, Schenectady, broadcast the inaugural ceremonies of Governor Alfred E. Smith.

If It Moves . . . Broadcast It

It was in 1923, too, that a former singer by the name of Graham McNamee, then a staff announcer of WJZ, got his first sports assignment—the broadcast of the World Series baseball games.

One epic broadcast followed another in rapid succession. KSD, St. Louis, accomplished a successful two-way pickup from a dirigible in flight.

KHJ, Los Angeles, and KGU in Honolulu teamed up for a transoceanic broadcast. WIP, Philadelphia, did a toyland parade. Memorial services for President Harding were heard over WRC, Washington.

WGN, the Chicago *Tribune* station, broadcast the entire Scopes evolution trial from Dayton, Tennessee, in 1925. At a cost of $1,000 a day, the court proceedings were picked up in their entirety. The courtroom was rearranged to accommodate the microphones, and listeners heard the testimony of witnesses and the cross-examinations and pleas of the two famous attorneys, Clarence Darrow and William Jennings Bryan.

That was the year that Gar Wood, the boatsman, decided to race the 20th Century Limited down a seventy-five mile stretch of the Hudson River. WGY, Schenectady, covered it.

Graham McNamee described Lindbergh's return to Washington, King George was heard welcoming delegates to the London Naval Conference, and Pope Pius XI addressed the world in an international broadcast inaugurating the Vatican City station, HVJ.

Special events were causing a great deal of concern in the offices of newspaper publishers where the press lords were hearing such things as the CBS eye-witness account of a fire inside the Ohio State Penitentiary as 318 lives were lost.

It Sounds Impossible

Adolf Ochs, publisher of the New York *Times*, got into the act himself and made radio history when he conversed on the air with Commander Richard E. Byrd in New Zealand where he had just arrived from his South Pole expedition.

It was on May 6, 1937, that the greatest special report in radio was made. Herb Morrison of WLS, Chicago, was at Lakehurst, New Jersey, doing a "routine" description of the landing of the German dirigible, the *Hindenburg*. As the mighty ship floated toward its mooring, Morrison began a pleasant word picture. Then tragedy struck. His words do not have the impact in print, but his sobbing description is one of the most moving broadcasts of all time:

The ship is gliding majestically toward us, like some great feather. We're standing here beside the American Airline flagships, waiting to rush them to all points of the United States when they get the ship moored. It's practically standing still—now they have dropped ropes out of the nose of the ship. The rain has slacked up a little bit. The back motors of the ship are just holding it . . . just enough to keep it from . . . (EXPLOSION) . . . *it's burst into flame!* Get this, Charlie! Get this, Charlie! It's crashing! Terrible! Oh my! Get out of the way please! It's burning—bursting into flame and it's falling on the mooring mast and . . . the folks . . . oh, this is terrible! This is one of the worst catastrophes in the world . . . oh, it's burning! (EXPLOSION) Oh, four or five hundred feet into the sky it's a terrific catastrophe ladies and gentlemen, (SOBS) it's smoke and flames now and the plane is crashing to the ground, not quite to the mooring mast . . . oh, the humanity. . . . " (HE IS CRYING)

In direct contrast to such coverage of epochal happenings, radio also had its cycle of broadcasts of oddball events. KDKA probably started it in 1934 when its listeners heard the sound of a heartbeat and a kiss.

The sound of Niagara Falls was picked up, and marriages by the score were performed on the air.

The first baby of the new year in Ogden, Utah, was "temporarily immortalized" on KLO. The microphone picked up the doctor's whack and the infant's first squall.

A little station in Laconia, New Hampshire, put a microphone next to a robin's nest for the exclusive sounds of a bird hatching. Patient engineers got it, too, from the first crack in the shell until the robin was halfway out.

In New York, WOR special-eventers fried an egg on the sidewalk one hot summer day, and later performed a wedding in a plane cruising over the city, with the wedding march piped in from a studio orchestra on the ground.

CBS had the first two-piano broadcast from a plane, with Peggy Keenan and Sandra Phillips, broadcasting melodies on two small nightclub pianos in a flying studio two miles above New York. The comedy team of Stoopnagel and Budd did a skit from the sky, "Stoop" in one plane, Budd in another.

"Round the Town," an elaborate, sponsored novelty program, used all the techniques learned over the years. It had Amelia Earhart and Ted Husing cruising over Manhattan and chatting with performers at various theaters and clubs. Eddie Duchin supplied the music from Central Park Casino, and DeWolf Hopper emoted atop the Empire State Building.

But if we should award a prize for the special event that required the most imagination, the most intricate setup, and the most insanity, it would go to station WHAS in Louisville for its "Radiogame."

It Sounds Impossible

The occasion was the 1925 World Series battle between the Pittsburgh Pirates and the Washington Senators. The WHAS brain trust hired Parkway Field in Louisville, enough idle ball players to make up two "sides," some official-looking umpires and a couple of referees. The idea was that one team would represent the Pirates and the other the Senators. Special wire reports of the actual play-by-play of the World Series were sent to the press box of the stadium in Louisville from wherever the series game of the day was being held—either Pittsburgh or Washington.

Are you ready? Two Louisville semipro teams, representing the series players, wore different uniforms decked out with big "P"s and "W"s to tell them apart. The instructions and directions of actual play were relayed to "actors" on the field . . . who ran through their parts with gusto. So while the series was being fought hundreds of miles away, Louisville fans were watching a very swinging tableau of the same action back home in ol' Kentucky.

Some of the baseball experts who watched this opening game pantomime in Louisville said it was as good as being at the series itself—maybe better.

Editor and Publisher said:

So faithfully were the big league plays duplicated that photographs taken at Forbes Field, Pittsburgh, and at Parkway Field, Louisville, were similar in nearly all respects.

Batters and runners could not hear the plays, but were coached by players on the various bases, all of whom were equipped with earphones. All bases were wired together, and all connected with the press box microphone. Each player was equipped with a complete wire device by which he received each play as called. This equipment could be detached when his team came in to bat and handed to the opposing player taking the field. An electrician was kept on hand to examine connections at the end of each inning and insure all players being "alive" at all times.

So well were the final two games timed that, starting a full inning behind the Washington game, the radio players caught up with the big leaguers in the last half of the seventh inning. During the eighth the announcer kept three plays behind Washington, in the ninth he sped by and kept one play behind. When the last Pirate batsman took his post the announcer caught up with Washington.

The crowds at Parkway Field, Louisville, and at Griffith Stadium, Washington, left the stands simultaneously.

Fans numbering 2,000 daily flocked to the Louisville field to see the games, despite cold raw wind and overcast skies.

Credo Fitch Harris, manager of WHAS, wrote this about the radiogame: "It really made a first-rate show, and our actor-players threw themselves into the act with unrestrained enthusiasm."

Special events are still a big part of broadcasting, although the egg hatchings, weddings, and egg-frying stunts are long gone. Yet, all these stunts played an important part in developing radio's versatility so that, years later, it would be standard operating procedure to broadcast the voice of a man circling the globe in a rocket.

Special events paved the way for the development of documentary programs, too.

Early in 1941, NBC presented one of the first network radio documentary series, "Defense for America," which combined and utilized past special-event pioneering.

Graham McNamee, along with a team of technicians, producers, reporters, and writers, went behind the guarded doors of America's defense industries and to Army, Navy, and Air Corps training camps in every part of the nation. "Through the magic of the microphone," to quote an NBC press release, "you hear the mighty roar of a nation preparing to defend its freedoms."

"Defense for America" was broadcast over ninety stations of the then NBC Red Network for thirty-nine weeks.

"Defense" had some unique aspects. First, there was a generous budget for lines, and this was vital to its success.

In 1941, all programs, or any part of a program, on a network had to be live.

There were no prerecordings, no such thing as tape, and naturally no prior editing. If you were broadcasting from a diving submarine, a moving tank, or a falling parachute—as was often the case on "Defense for America"—the pickup had to be instantaneous. This was a bonanza for the telephone company. Facilities budget on a single program often exceeded $5,000. Such remote originations involved miles of new line construction, days of engineering time, and ulcer-breeding pauses until an intelligible signal was obtained.

This idiotic network ruling made programs like "Defense for America" almost prohibitively expensive, did nothing to improve its content, and created fantastic problems for the broadcaster.

For example, the twentieth broadcast of "Defense for America" told the story of cotton, from the plantation to the mills, and ultimately to its usefulness in national defense.

The program opened with an interview with Will Jeter, a cotton farmer living some sixty miles south of Atlanta. The microphone was actually in the center of a cotton field, so Jeter could describe the planting, cultivation, and picking of cotton.

To arrange this, all long-distance phone service to a nearby Georgia village was suspended for about six minutes. Naturally, the phone company would not assume this responsibility. Permission was granted after the writer took a trip to the town and spent several bourbon-tinted hours with the mayor. But verbal permission was not acceptable to the NBC lawyers. They required a letter. This was obtained only five hours before airtime. The contents of the letter were phoned to New York, and finally, just twenty minutes before the broadcast, NBC permission was received. A nice comfortable atmosphere, indeed, in which to rehearse a very nervous and barely articulate Georgia cotton farmer.

The switch to and from the farm was on a "time cue." The director decided to open this scene with the ringing of a huge iron bell, used to denote hours to field hands. He threw in a little group singing, too.

The director was a hard worker—a most intense man, and intent on throwing hand cues correctly he accidentally knocked his stopwatch into a well. This broadcast segment was supposed to last exactly eight minutes, and the poor guy had to guess at the time.

The program then switched to Fort Benning, Georgia, for a description of parachute training. The highspot here was Graham McNamee broadcasting his sensations as he did a 500-foot drop in a parachute from the training tower.

Mac had a hand mike with a long cable attached. As he descended, a jeep was supposed to drive away from the tower, pulling the cable free of the chute. When Mac started down, the jeep's motor conked out, and the car wouldn't budge. Fortunately, three soldiers grabbed the cable lead and tugged it across the field, without snapping the microphone connections.

Three additional remote spots were equally precarious, but managed to get on the air.

That evening a half-dozen exhausted, harried broadcasters were discussing the day's problems over a light libation in a hotel room. They asked the telephone operator to place long-distance calls to NBC, New York, their various homes in the East, the site of the next broadcast, St. Louis, and the War Department in Washington.

But the calls didn't get through. A half-hour later, when the local sheriff rapped on the door, they understood why. The hotel operator had decided that only a "flock of drunks" would attempt that many long-distance calls.

Yet these hectic, exciting, strenuous, frustrated days of the first documentaries built a firm foundation for today. It was this kind of experimentation that helped make possible such shows as "One World," "Person to Person," "The 20th Century," "David Brinkley's Journal," and the slick documentaries we enjoy now.

CHAPTER 6

It's Okay, Mom, I Won!

T H E wedding of broadcasting and sports events took place on April 11, 1921. They were made for each other, although, as in any marriage, there were serious doubts about it for a while. It seemed reasonable to assume that if you could sit home and listen to a fight, there was no particular incentive to hie yourself down to the nearest ticket broker and slap down the price of a ducat to a boxing bout. However, in the beginning, sports promoters looked at radio as merely something which might conceivably give a bout a little more publicity, and perhaps some prestige.

The Pittsburgh *Post*'s sports editor, Florent Gibson, did the first play-by-play sports event of record over KDKA. It was the no-decision Johnny Ray versus Johnny Dundee fight at Pittsburgh's Motor Square Garden. This was the first blow-by-blow description in history, and its success started some top people in the industry thinking about sports and radio.

It Sounds Impossible

David Sarnoff had just been named general manager of the new Radio Corporation of America, and had conceived the idea of broadcasting the world's heavyweight boxing championship between titleholder Jack Dempsey—who had defeated Jess Willard at Toledo just two years before—and French challenger Georges Carpentier.

The Frenchman had become a glamorous figure in sporting and theatrical circles throughout the world, and Dempsey, the Manassa Mauler, was probably more popular than the President of the United States. The bout had wonderful international ramifications. It was a true world championship. The date for the fight was set for July 2, 1921.

Boyle's Thirty Acres in Jersey City was chosen as the site for the event—which caused a few problems for David Sarnoff. KDKA was the only commercial broadcasting station in the country at that time, and RCA had no claim on its facilities. Also, it was too far from Jersey City to be of any use. But Sarnoff went ahead anyway.

He called Major J. Andrew White, the editor of a radio publication called *Wireless Age,* and asked him to arrange for the broadcast of the fight.

White called in two radio technicians, Harry Walker and J. O. Smith, to handle the technical details.

White discovered that the General Electric Company had just finished building a transmitter intended for the Navy—but hadn't delivered it yet. He succeeded in borrowing it. White also proved his promotional prowess by talking the officials of the Lackawanna Railroad into stringing an aerial between their two experimental train wireless towers in Hoboken. White, too, talked the Pullman porters of the road into letting him use the shack in which they changed into their uniforms for their trips. Into their galvanized-iron dressing room he moved a ton of radio equipment.

The broadcast was carried over a two-station hookup on WJZ, Newark, and WGY, Schenectady.

It worked extremely well even though Smith, who was operating the transmitter, almost went blind from standing too close to the glaring tubes that sent out White's blow-by-blow description.

The best estimate is that 300,000 owners of crystal sets and one-tube radios heard White describe Dempsey's knockout of Carpentier in the fourth round—heard him tell about the challenger breaking his thumb against the champ's jaw—heard him describe the orderliness of the 90,000 people gathered in the wooden saucer at Boyle's Thirty Acres.

The lid was off—and it was a milestone for two men who were literally to shape the destinies of two great networks. David Sarnoff later founded the National Broadcasting Company, and Major White played a vital role in the formation of the Columbia Broadcasting System.

In early August KDKA broadcast the play-by-play detail of the Davis Cup Tennis Matches in which an Australian team defeated the British at Pittsburgh's Allegheny Country Club in suburban Sewickley.

The 1921 World Series was an all–New York affair, with the Giants meeting the Yankees at the Polo Grounds. The opener came on October 5th, and KDKA, with a direct wire to Pittsburgh, had the famous sportswriter Grantland Rice at the microphone.

KDKA, too, made baseball scores available to listeners regularly.

It Sounds Impossible

Out in Chicago, WGN began broadcasting Midwestern football games on a regular basis, and for the first time had its microphones at the 500-mile speedway classic at Indianapolis.

The Big Three of America's sportscasters in 1929 were Graham McNamee, Ted Husing, and Bill Munday. Both "Mac" and Ted are gone now, but Munday, who is considered the Dean of American Sports Announcers, is still on the air with the University of Georgia football games.

Bill Stern, Clem McCarthy, Red Barber, Mel Allen, Tom Harmon, Red Grange, Lindsay Nelson, and Chris Schenkel came along later in the chronology of sports in radio.

Slate knew both McNamee and Munday well. He recalls:

* * *

Bill Munday and I went to the University of Georgia together. He graduated a couple of years ahead of me, but we belonged to the same fraternity and were friends.

Bill was a big, handsome blond boy—quite articulate and very inventive. He was an indifferent southpaw in baseball, but a very active campus correspondent for the Atlanta *Journal*. And he was his own best press agent.

Once he got a press photographer to take a very dramatic picture of himself in his Georgia baseball outfit—his left foot raised high in the air, his right arm almost touch-ing the ground, and a look of "surprised pain" on his southern kisser.

He wrote the caption himself. It said:

"Ace lefty Bill Munday of the Georgia Bulldogs throwing his famous pitch that defies the laws of gravity!"

The Associated Press distributed the picture, and within

It's Okay, Mom, I Won!

a week and a half a dozen big-league scouts were in Athens to investigate this phenomenon. They weren't too happy to discover that the team used Bill primarily for batting practice and an occasional unimportant game.

In those days Bill never dreamed of becoming a sportscaster. He wanted to be a newspaper sportswriter—which he became, and a good one, too—for the Atlanta *Journal*.

Yet, at the time he received—unwittingly—training that proved very valuable in his radio future.

The Negro butler at the Sigma Nu house was a privileged and an interesting character. He was known as "Brother" Dougherty—and he was really more member than servant. On Sundays he became "Reverend" Dougherty, and was the visiting preacher at scores of nearby churches. In fact, "Reverend" Dougherty became such an excellent preacher, and his pulpit appearances were so in demand, that a few years later he resigned the fraternity house to become a full-time divine. Bill Munday was largely responsible.

And Brother Dougherty was partly responsible for Bill's success as a broadcaster.

On Saturday nights Bill would prepare Brother Dougherty's sermons. Armed with a dictionary, a copy of Roget's thesaurus, Bartlett's quotations, a Bible, and his own inimitable knack of turning a phrase, Bill would rehearse the good brother for hours. He'd write part of the sermon, instruct the Reverend Dougherty in its delivery, timing, and emphasis. He was both voice coach and work supplier. The demand for Dougherty's services increased each month. And Bill was gaining the finest possible training for broadcasting.

When Bill Munday started broadcasting sports events,

the most famous scribes in the country paid him compliments. Paul Gallico, in the New York *Daily News* of July 29, 1929, said:

"Suddenly from the loud speaker . . . comes a fresh new voice, a voice that for all its Southern cadances and rhythmics is letting fly a bristling, rapid fire of description, couched in a new and gay phraseology, teeming with good humor and enthusiasm, and demonstrating without ostentation how sports on radio should be spoken."

Graham McNamee really became a national figure with the 1927 Rose Bowl game. It was the first coast-to-coast hookup, and millions listened to Mac's exciting and thrilling description of the 7 to 7 tie between Alabama and Stanford.

"Mac," as he was called by his friends, had a real Jekyll and Hyde personality. Most times, Mac was kind, considerate, very patient with his admirers, and a great companion, but he was always conscious of the fact that he was "Mister Radio" to millions of Americans. He demanded and expected preferential treatment, and if he didn't get it . . . well! Mac didn't care who was involved—NBC vice presidents, hotel managers, head writers, advertising or corporate executives, Army or Navy brass. With his distinctive voice, excellent diction sprinkled with sarcasm, invective and ascerbic phrases, Mac was seldom topped in an argument.

His voice was easy to recognize, and over the years pictures of Mac had been printed thousands of times in newspapers and magazines. He narrated one of the major newsreels, and his face appeared weekly on movie screens throughout the United States.

Mac can aptly be described as lantern-jawed. His long

face, big mouth, and deep voice gave the impression of a tall man, but he was well under six feet.

I've heard dozens of people, on first meeting Mac, say, "But I thought you were a much bigger man." This irritated him far more than any other comment.

He was generally very gracious to autograph seekers. I once saw him miss a train in Detroit rather than disappoint some fifty school students who wanted his signature. But he detested them at mealtimes, especially so in a Pullman diner.

Someone would stop at the table and say, "Aren't you Graham McNamee?"

He would slowly place his knife and fork on the plate, and in a grating, squeaky voice reply, "Now, really! Am I as ugly as that fast-talking son of a bitch?" or if it were a woman, Mac would say, "Madame, I'm the Reverend Sam Slate." (He always used the name of one of his companions.) "I do not approve of people in show business and I shall ask God to forgive you for such a grievous error." This one always brought a stumbling apology.

Yet, Mac loved to talk to people, especially women, regardless of their age or pulchritude. Once, as a favor to me, he attended a wedding in a small southern town. He was particularly charming to two elderly ladies. After the wedding he insisted on taking them to dinner. They had a wonderful time, and spoke of having dinner with "that nice Mr. McNamee" for years. One of them was my mother.

In Buffalo, Mac's interest in two bright, attractive girls probably saved the lives of four people. We checked out of the Statler Hotel and were having a casual drink before going to the airport for the 11:00 P.M. flight to Chicago. Mac decided he'd buy a nightcap and tell one more story.

It Sounds Impossible

We told him we were afraid we'd miss the plane, so Mac phoned the airport and switched our reservations to the midnight flight. We were tired and more than slightly annoyed with Mac. Later we discovered that the 11:00 P.M. flight had crashed on takeoff. There were no survivors.

By 1924 there were three million radio homes tuning in to over two hundred stations. With sports events the hottest ticket radio was offering to date, and sports promoters being quick to note the potential of that vast unseen audience, there was much head scratching to see what could be done to protect the promoter's investment in his "live" gate and capitalize on the radio audience at the same time.

An incident in Boston helped the broadcasters not at all in trying to prove that radio helped *increase* rather than *decrease* the size of a sporting event box-office gate.

Violinist Fritz Kreisler, the concert circuit's biggest draw, was booked into a Boston hall seating three thousand people. The concert was a sellout—until it was announced that the event was to be broadcast. Fifteen hundred tickets were returned.

Too, the record companies were making loud noises about *their* sales being off because of radio.

When a sports promoter had a bum gate and a broadcast on the same night, he of course blamed it all on radio —not on the card.

While radio stations were not too eager to get into the business of buying what the promoters called "broadcast rights," the sponsors and potential sponsors saw a merchandising gold mine in the underwriting of sports events on the air.

The nation's Number One sports promoter of the day was dapper Tex Rickard, who booked the biggest boxing bouts. He was the man who matched Carpentier and Dempsey, Willard and Dempsey. He was the king of Madison Square Garden. Naturally, he watched radio's impact on sports with much concern.

Actually, there was no such thing as a sponsored fight until 1926 when the Royal Typewriter Company entered negotiations with Mr. Rickard.

Royal started by offering $15,000 for rights per fight.

Rickard started a little higher—at $40,000 a fight, claiming that his gate would suffer drastically.

Royal went up a little, and Rickard came down a lot. They compromised at $20,000.

The matter of "rights" had a precedent—and sports events were "in" as standard and very popular radio fare.

Today, radio and television rights run into the millions for professional baseball and football, collegiate football, pro fights and golf, and no one—including the Gillette Safety Razor Company—bats an eye.

To be sure, for a really big event the city of the point of origin is "blacked out," showing that the old bugaboo "live gateitis" still bothers the promoters, but sports is still a tremendous draw in radio-TV programming. It always will be.

The nations sportscasters, too, have left a jargon of their own to spice American phraseology.

It'll be a long time before we forget the late Clem McCarthy's guttural, rolling "A-a-and they're off!" at the start of the Kentucky Derby . . . or Dizzy Dean's murder of the language, including his famous ". . . and he slud into third."

Who remembers the name of the fighter who first said, "It's all right, Mom; I won!"?

It was right after the Dave Shade–Jimmy Slattery fight

at the New York Polo Grounds in 1925. Nils T. Granlund was the sportscaster for Station WHN (which later became WMGM, which later became WHN again). After the fight Granlund climbed into the ring with his big carbon microphone and pushed it into the face of the winner—Shade. Little David put a new phrase into the American language.

CHAPTER 7

The Big Hookup

SOMEWHERE in the dim past of talking pictures, on some shelf in some Hollywood vault, there is, on film, a scene between round-faced, wise-cracking Jack Oakie and a Hollywood hero-type. Oakie is all wrapped up in radio gear. Both are bone-tired. They have been working day and night for what seems to be *years* to give the public the first broadcast of a championship prizefight—and at this moment they have succeeded. If memory serves, they are lamenting the fact that only a few thousand people heard the fight. The hero-type grins and muses something like, "Wouldn't it be great if we could connect up a whole lot of stations and broadcast over all of them at the same time?"

Oakie's head snaps up. His eyes shine. He snaps his fingers. He looks skyward. "Wow! What a sensational idea!" he says.

Network broadcasting had been kicking around in the minds of radio engineers and executives for many years.

Actually, the engineering staff of American Telephone

and Telegraph Company had been struggling with the problem of multiple-station transmission since 1923. They kept coming back to one rather obvious conclusion—that the answer to interconnecting stations lay in the principle of the long-distance phone call, using "long" lines on which to carry the programs.

The first "network" was tried out on January 4, 1923, when WEAF, New York, and WNAC, Boston, were connected by telephone wire, and carried identical broadcasts at the same time. AT&T learned that a special high-efficiency cable was needed in carrying talk, music, and the broad range of broadcast sounds from station to station with enough fidelity to rebroadcast it. There was also the small problem of amplification. After all, how much sound could one cram down a cable?

By June of 1923 they had developed the type of line needed and, at a meeting of the National Electric Light Association in New York City, they conducted their second formal demonstration. The key station was again WEAF, New York, but this time they tied in WGY, Schenectady; KDKA, Pittsburgh; and KYW, Chicago. A specially produced program was broadcast from the Association banquet on the night of June 7th, with WEAF originating and feeding the show to the other three stations. Success.

The fact of simultaneous broadcasts all over the country probably was not the main motivating factor in the development of network radio. Some rather important things were happening to radio economically—and to other businesses. By 1925 the arguments were still heated as to whether radio helped or hurt actors at the boxoffice. Nightclub operators were smiling and reporting that, by putting their floor-show stars on the radio, they were cleaning up.

The Big Hookup

But the famous tenor John McCormack withdrew from radio when he found his record sales going down and his box-office receipts at concerts dwindling.

Antiradio factions were stirring up little storms about radio being overcommercial—an argument to hound the medium with growing intensity. Some cities were writing ordinances about radio's indiscriminate use by set owners. In certain instances radio was called a public nuisance. Operators of motion-picture theaters, according to an ancient story in *Variety,* needled radio on their local screens. At the Senate Theatre in Chicago the manager encouraged his organist to work up a scornful theme in a solo with slides. He did, and as he played a sign flashed on the screen that read, "You're a nut if you listen to radio programs!"

As the "threat" of network radio grew, so did opposition to radio by the record companies, music publishers, vaudeville and motion-picture theaters. Newspapers climbed into the ring, and literally thousands of them refused to carry "free radio advertising."

Regardless of what side of the radio fence you were on in 1925, one thing was certain—radio was becoming a large economic entity in the United States, and there didn't seem to be much anyone could do to retard its growth.

By 1926 the National Broadcasting Company had been formed, although their first coast-to-coast operations were not to begin until 1928. NBC took over what was then called "The Red Network." It was a chain of about twenty stations which had begun back in 1923 with a New York to Providence hookup between two stations—WEAF and WJAR.

Actually, owning a radio network consists, primarily, of having enough cash to lease telephone lines from

AT&T, some programming, a financial repayment deal that will interest prospective affiliates, and the business acumen to be able to sell your programs to advertisers. How simple can life be?

In NBC's case, the investment in lines alone ran into millions—but David Sarnoff had more than a notion about the impact of stations in all major cities broadcasting the same program at the same time. Never had the conception of mass media been so massive.

To assure a New York outlet for its programs, NBC bought station WEAF from American Telephone for the then fabulous amount of a million dollars.

NBC took a full-page ad in New York and other papers to announce the event. It read, in part:

ANNOUNCING THE
NATIONAL BROADCASTING COMPANY, INC.

National radio broadcasting with better programs permanently assured by this important action of the Radio Corporation of America in the interest of the listening public.

WEAF Purchased
for $1,000,000

The Radio Corporation of America, therefore, is interested, just as the public is, in having the most adequate programs broadcast. It is interested, as the public is, in having them comprehensive and free from discrimination.

Any use of radio transmission which causes the public to feel that the quality of the programs is not the highest, that the use of radio is not the broadest and best use in the public

The Big Hookup

interest, that it is used for political advantage or selfish power, will be detrimental to the public interest in radio, and therefore to the Radio Corporation of America.

To insure, therefore, the development of this great service, the Radio Corporation of America has purchased for one million dollars station WEAF from the American Telephone and Telegraph Company, that company having decided to retire from the broadcasting business.

National Broadcasting Company Organized

The Radio Corporation of America has decided to incorporate that station, which has achieved such a deservedly high reputation for the quality and character of its programs, under the name of the National Broadcasting Company, Inc.

The Purpose of the New Company

The purpose of that company will be to provide the best programs available for broadcasting in the United States.

The National Broadcasting Company will not only broadcast these programs through station WEAF, but it will make them available to other broadcasting stations throughout the country so far as it may be practicable to do so, and they may desire to take them.

It is hoped that arrangements may be made so that every event of national importance may be broadcast widely throughout the United States.

M. H. Aylesworth to Be President

It Sounds Impossible

The President of the New National Broadcasting Company will be M. H. Aylesworth, for many years Managing Director of the National Electric Light Association. He will perform the executive and administrative duties of the corporation.

Mr. Aylesworth, while not hitherto identified with the radio industry or broadcasting, has had public experience as Chairman of the Colorado Public Utilities Commission, and through his work with the association which represents the electrical industry, has a broad understanding of the technical problems which measure the pace of broadcasting.

We have no hesitation in recommending the National Broadcasting Company to the people of the United States.

Aylesworth introduced the inaugural broadcast over twenty-four stations from the grand ballroom of the Waldorf-Astoria Hotel on the night of November 15, 1926.

The lineup of stars was tremendous. Never before had such an array of talent appeared on one show.

Will Rogers, at the very peak of his popularity, was "picked up" from Kansas City; Mary Garden was heard "direct" from Chicago. Both received a fee of $2,500. Eddie Cantor got $1,500 for his comedy routine from New York. The total talent bill ran over $25,000, and the lineup included Weber and Fields, the greatest comedy team of the day; Walter Damrosch and the New York Symphony, Albert Stoessel and the New York Oratorio Society, Titta Ruffo, the famous Metropolitan Opera baritone; and the dance orchestras of Vincent Lopez, George Olsen, Ben Bernie, and B. A. Rolfe. Edwin Franko Goldman's band played marches and concert music, and the Gilbert and Sullivan Light Opera Company rounded out the evening with song.

The program began at 8:00 P.M. and ran until midnight. The thousand newspaper people, stage and screen stars, and political celebrities in the ballroom were genuinely awed by the spectacle.

Uncounted hundreds of thousands heard it on crystal sets and new loudspeaker radios as far west as Minneapolis and St. Paul.

Will Rogers was quoted after the broadcast as saying, "Radio is too big a thing to be out of!"

Competition to NBC was not long in coming.

The formation of the new network was not so simple as NBC's. The route leading up to the actual existence of the Columbia Broadcasting System was a circuitous one.

It began, really, with a call on David Sarnoff by a man named Arthur Judson who had been manager of the Philadelphia Orchestra and had, by then, formed his own concert management and booking agency. The purpose of Judson's call upon Sarnoff—just before NBC began broadcasting—was to talk about his artists appearing on sponsored programs for a fee.

Like most bookers, he was resisting the practice of local stations asking performers to appear for "publicity" only. Sarnoff asked Judson to prepare a plan for paying artists, which Judson submitted to him early in 1926.

Judson claims that Sarnoff liked the plan, and Judson assumed Sarnoff would put him in charge of programs when—and if—Sarnoff began operating the broadcast chain.

What Judson didn't know was that NBC was already being built and that Sarnoff was not planning to use Judson's services. Judson organized his own program company in the fall of 1926, and, along with a promoter named George Coats, was ready to offer NBC musical entertainment at a price.

It Sounds Impossible

It didn't work out, and Judson decided to challange the NBC "monopoly." Sarnoff had just signed a contract with AT&T for almost all available long lines for broadcast, and suggested that even if Judson had a broadcasting station—which he didn't—he couldn't have a network without wires.

Judson organized his own "chain" anyway. United Independent Broadcasters was a protest against what Judson called "the RCA monopoly."

United it was—but broadcasting it wasn't. He added another associate to his cause in the person of J. Andrew White—the man who made history with his description of the Dempsey-Carpentier fight.

Another promoter-newspaperman named H. H. Newman was brought in, and the four divided a thousand shares of stock.

Coats was sent on the road to try to sign up stations for the network, and by the time he had signed eleven they were able to convince the owners of the Bamberger station in Newark—WOR—that they should sign for a year as the New York outlet for the network.

By 1927 the new chain had the stations but no wires.

Coats was able to make some contacts in Washington. Although the telephone company told him at first that it might take three years to furnish lines, he was able to report very shortly to Judson by telegram that he "had the wires."

Because the foursome figured it would take about $100,000 a month to operate the system, they looked desperately for capital to keep them afloat. They began to negotiate with the Victor Talking Machine Company to come in as a partner, but things suddenly skidded to a stop when RCA took over Victor.

The Big Hookup

They went to the Columbia Phonograph Corporation, and were successful in getting the firm to take over the operating broadcasting rights of the independent chain for an initial payment amounting to a little over $150,000.

The name was changed to the Columbia Phonograph Broadcasting System and was operated under a contract allowing Columbia to cancel out on thirty days' notice.

By the time the chain opened—on September 19, 1927—they had sold *one* commercial hour.

The first month was disaster in red ink. All loss, no gain. White, Coats, Newman, and Judson went scrambling for additional cash, and finally turned up enough to keep the network afloat for another few weeks.

Then Coats approached a multimillionaire he had heard of by the name of Jerome Louchheim who was in the contracting business in Philadelphia and was rated at about $20,000,000. After many long talks with Coats, Louchheim finally decided to go along, and bought controlling interest in the network.

Just as things began to brighten up, WOR, the New York outlet, announced that it didn't have much faith in chain broadcasting, and wouldn't renew its contract. New radio licenses were scarce in the New York area, but Columbia found a struggling little station in Steinway Hall, New York City, whose owners were willing to listen. All they had, really, was a license to operate. The price may have seemed high—but Columbia needed a New York outlet. So it was that WABC (later to become WCBS) became the first station acquired by the new network.

Still in financial straits by trying to compete with the healthy and wealthy NBC, more stock had to be sold and new avenues of investment income opened up.

One big problem was the deal that Columbia made

with its first sixteen affiliates. The network had agreed to purchase ten hours a week from each station at the rate of $50 an hour. Where to find sponsors to pay this $8,000-a-week nut along with all the other costs was a problem of considerable magnitude—to say the least. Major White toured the stations of the network and secured more reasonable contracts. But, even so, losses were mounting.

Enter William Samuel Paley of Philadelphia, Pennsylvania.

One of the very few Columbia-network sponsors was the Congress Cigar Company. Congress had been selling La Palina cigars on radio with a program called "The La Palina Smoker," and the statistical incident that showed the sales of La Palina cigars jumping from 400,000 to 1,000,000 a day caused the company's advertising manager, twenty-seven-year-old Bill Paley, to generate some genuine enthusiasm about broadcasting. When he learned that CBS was for sale, he persuaded some associates to join him in buying it.

Records show that Paley bought the then puny network for $400,000.

The gross billings of CBS in 1927 were $72,500.

Paley immediately surrounded himself with people he felt could make this venture pay off both economically and artistically. Major White stayed on as managing director until 1930. Arthur Judson merged seven concert bureaus into a firm called Columbia Concerts Corporation. The idea here was to ensure the network plenty of talent—which was really Judson's main idea in the first place.

Paley persuaded a Federal Radio Commissioner, Sam Pickard, to resign his appointment and join him as vice-president in charge of station relations. He recruited Edward Klauber, night city editor of *The New York Times,* and later made him executive vice-president. He sought out operational talent with an eye to public service and advertising acumen.

After rearranging the capital structure of CBS, the young network president formed a Hollywood alliance that would give the network access to motion-picture talent. It was a sort of stock swap whereby half the CBS stock shares went to Paramount-Publix Corporation in exchange for 59,000 shares of the movie company's stock, but for the time being it gave him some great bargaining advantages with talent . . . as NBC was soon to find out.

In fact, Paley was to become a large entity in a very short time in network broadcasting—a real competition to NBC, and often a thorn in the side of the older network.

CHAPTER 8

Radio's Royalty

IF RADIO programming ever had a monarch, it was John Royal. We had been invited to his office where he still held forth as consultant to NBC. It was August, 1962. "Let's," Royal had suggested on the phone, "get a few facts straight."

We welcomed the relief from the sun as we walked under the long brick-red canopy at 30 Rockefeller Plaza and ducked into the cool dark reaches of the RCA Building. We didn't walk to the studio "side" of the building, but headed for the front bank of elevators that would take us to the "ivory tower" area of the National Broadcasting Company. Some unromantic building operator put the offices of NBC's President Kintner and his top aides on the mere sixth floor of a building that boasts seventy stories.

But you know where you are when you step off the elevator and walk over the heavily carpeted area to the sixth floor's first reception desk. The quiet is almost overwhelming compared to the frantic activity of some of the studio areas on the other side of the house. This is vice-presidentland.

On the way up we wondered how many aspiring radio and television stars—and their agents and their lawyers—had cooled their heels waiting to see John Royal over the last thirty-some years.

The outer area was empty. No one was waiting. The receptionist behind the sleek, rubbed wood desk told us that we were expected and that Mr. Royal's office was down the corridor, just past Mr. Kintner's, and to go right in.

We had met John Royal several times in the past, but this time we looked at him with an eye to describing the man that many of the world's greatest stars called "Mr. Radio."

Today he is the tall, husky, white-haired, well-tanned prototype of the network senior vice-president in charge of charting the destinies of stars. The voice is heavy and positive. The important words are underlined with resonance that fills the room and leaves no question as to what Mr. Royal means or doesn't mean. The laugh is hearty and the manner is friendly.

He didn't sit behind his desk for our talk, but moved over to a big leather chair beside it.

Before he came to New York in February of 1931, John Royal had been a newspaper reporter and a public-relations man. He was the press agent for the great Houdini. Another of his early accounts was the Boston Opera Company. Then he ran some of the big theaters of the Keith-Albee chain in Boston and Cincinnati, and the big Hippodrome in Cleveland.

Royal had gone into commercial radio in 1928 as vice-president and general manager of WTAM in Cleveland.

WTAM was an NBC affiliate, and the network had a great deal of regard for Royal's business ability. "Respect" is probably a better word. In attempting to renegotiate a contract with WTAM, NBC told Royal that it could pay nowhere near the $50 an hour he was asking the network for time on the station. Perhaps a percentage of the rate card, they suggested.

"I told them to go to hell." Royal laughed. "I wanted $50 an hour."

NBC bought the station, and offered Royal a job in New York.

"I told them 'no' again," Royal said. "I didn't want any part of New York. But I took a trip out here and had a meeting with Deac Aylesworth. We talked, and he took me over to 711 Fifth Avenue where NBC had its studios, and I met some of the people. But I didn't like New York. It seemed too big for me. Maybe I worried about living among all these so-called sophisticated people. I don't know.

"Aylesworth made me a fairly attractive offer and asked me to think it over.

"I took a taxi to Grand Central Station. I was ready to go back to the Midwest. When I got to the station, I saw this big crowd standing around looking up. They were watching a guy named Shipwreck Kelly sitting on top of a flagpole. Not only that: I saw people actually paying ten cents apiece to look at this mug through a telescope! So I called Deac on the phone and told him I had made up my mind to take the job and come to New York."

"Why?"

"I told him that if people are silly enough to pay ten cents to see this fella sitting on a flagpole, New York is the place for me!"

Radio's Royalty

New York and Royal were made for each other, for Royal was above all things a showman.

One of his earliest concerns was the physical studio setup at 711 Fifth Avenue. The studios themselves were as well appointed as any radio studios could be. But after all, reasoned Royal, what is a radio studio? It's a room. There are drapes and wall hangings, a few chairs and a piano. In the middle of the room is an upright pipe holding a tin can. This is it.

"How could we invite a prospective advertiser to a studio and suggest he spend a million dollars in originating a program from this room? I was of the theater, and there you had the glamour—the proscenium arch, the multi-colored lights, the scenery, the dressing rooms, the smell of greasepaint, the vast auditorium—and the girls. God bless them, the girls."

Royal immediately employed a bevy of Ziegfeld Follies-type girls to populate the studios of NBC. They were taught enough about the mechanics of network broadcasting to be able to answer questions and conduct informal tours of the premises when advertisers, visiting dignitaries, and just plain visitors appeared on the scene. This operation was the forerunner of a very successful adjunct to NBC's service—the Radio City guided tour, which today still boasts of the prettiest guidettes and handsomest pages in town.

"It sure took the advertiser's mind off the bareness of the room," Royal commented.

But Royal's big job was to build programs and corral stars.

"In the early days, around 1930 and 1931," Royal said, "RCA had a deal with RKO, and part of the arrangement was to give them one hour every Friday night. It was to be called 'The RKO Hour.' Of course, everything in those days was the something-hour. 'The Palmolive Hour,' 'The Eveready Hour,' 'The Atwater Kent Hour.' Everything was an hour. Actually, the fifteen-minute program, the half-hour show, all were simple divisions of 'the hour.' It was nobody's *idea* to make programs this length. It just happened. Just as great lineups of shows just 'happened' in the early days.

"In the beginning, nobody decided it would be a great thought to have a strong bloc of programs back-to-back on a given night. It happened accidentally on NBC, and when we saw what kind of captive audience it gave us we began thinking in these terms. There were three hour-long shows on our network on a Thursday night. It was a mistake, really. The agencies and clients all wanted that audience—they couldn't get together—we ended up with an entertainment package for listeners that was a powerhouse. Only, it took a while to realize it.

"But back to that 'RKO Hour.' These artists were supposed to come over here to put on a vaudeville show taken from the acts at RKO theaters. So they put on radio the acts they were using in the theaters. And they died. Their material wasn't adjusted—it was terrible for radio.

"One big trouble was audience reaction—the thing that Ed Wynn went through. At first they weren't allowed to have any audience at all; then small audiences were let in. Our engineering brain trust told the visitors that while they were in the halls they were not to move. They should not applaud or laugh. There could be no vibration. So the audiences were scared to do anything."

Eddie Cantor was another pioneer in getting the audience to help take the onus off the radio performer when he asked John Royal, "How can we get laughs if we don't let the audience laugh?"

"By the time we moved from 711 Fifth Avenue to Radio City," Royal said, "we were educated. We made a place for the audience in big variety shows. Of *course* comedians had to have an audience that laughed, and musical acts needed applause. We removed the glass curtain between the performer and the studio audience. The quality of the entertainment seemed to improve immediately."

Later, radio producers were to learn that another strange phenomenon had occurred without their knowing it. The listening audience was developing an "association" with the audience in the studio, and people in living rooms from coast to coast were laughing out loud while they were listening to the radio.

The big problem in Royal's early days was not money to pay the talent; it was material. The biggest name in the theater then was his former boss, crusty Edward F. Albee, who ran the gigantic Keith-Albee Circuit. Only William Morris, the Shuberts, and Marcus Loew were real threats to this tremendous talent empire. Albee controlled a lot of stars, and would not allow his performers to broadcast on the radio. The delightful irony of Albee's stand against radio is that within ten years his company bore the radio label. Keith-Albee had become Radio-Keith-Orpheum.

"So," Royal said, "it rapidly became apparent that we were going to have to invent our own people and develop material specially suited for radio."

"Amos 'n' Andy" was a good example of that. Here was a team *made* for broadcasting. They weren't the usual baggy-pants, black-face rube comics who blew all their material in a few minutes. They developed the comedy serial. "Actually," Royal said, the team of Amos 'n' Andy gave the audience very little in that fifteen minutes a night. You could relax listening to them. They didn't force a lot of humor on you. They never gave too much—just eased along. And this was their secret. They were real students of entertaining by radio, and they were conscientious. No one was allowed in their studio. They took the delineation of their characters most seriously—and they succeeded."

So well, in fact, that even the President of the United States, Calvin Coolidge, didn't want to be bothered when "Amos 'n' Andy" was on.

But by and large, performers wanted to get on the broadcasting bandwagon because it was the talk of the times. There was still something quite mysterious and glamorous about putting a voice on the air.

"There was something else," Royal said, "that artists were hearing about—a new breed of fan. Until then it was pretty common knowledge among the artists that good publicity pictures in the papers could do a lot to create a following. Everybody was aware that a sexy photo would do a lot for a girl's career. There was the 'It' girl, Clara Bow; and there were Greta Garbo, Joan Crawford, and Jean Harlow. All of them knew the value of a well-placed publicity still. But nobody was ready for the effect of a *man's voice* on a woman! This was unbelievable! Women went mad over the voices of Jimmy Wallington, Graham McNamee, Norman Brokenshire—any of our deep-throated he-men.

"The barrage of sexy mail they got was ridiculous. At first, many of the letters were written in pencil, and a lot of them had RFD addresses, but as the announcers became better known and the programs became more exciting, the letters became more urban. They were in pen and ink, and even typewritten. Often perfumed.

"I had been at NBC only a year or so when some crackpot called my office and asked me if I knew Graham McNamee. I said sure—McNamee works for us. The guy told me to have McNamee in my office at eight o'clock that night because he was going to come up and kill him!

"I asked him why—and he said that his wife had gone dippy over McNamee's voice and was making his marriage miserable. Needless to say, I didn't have McNamee within ten miles of my office that night, but this nut didn't show up."

Often, however, the lady's ardor was dampened when she saw her favorite radio star in person. Royal told of a traveling salesman who had a serious domestic problem when his wife went gaga over a WTAM announcer. Royal invited his friend to bring his wife to Cleveland to watch a couple of broadcasts. Her idol's sexy, resonant tones didn't overcome his no-chin ugly mug, and the woman was completely disillusioned. The next day the salesman called Royal with profuse thanks.

Some great shows made their NBC debut under John Royal's aegis. On September 27, 1931, "The Lady Esther Serenade" began. Who remembers Harry Horlick and "The A&P Gypsies"? Joe Penner stepped into radio and made the phrase "Ya' wanna buy a duck?" a household word. Ozzie Nelson supplied the music for Penner's Sunday-night show—and rumor had it the curlyheaded maestro was in love with, and might marry, his pretty girl-singer, Harriet Hilliard. He did.

It Sounds Impossible

Brand names began popping up in show titles—"The Atwater Kent Entertainers," "Silvertown Cord Orchestra," "The Eagle Neutrodyne Hour," "The Ipana Troubadors," "Billy Jones and Ernie Hare—The Interwoven Pair"!

Royal brought Gene and Glenn to radio. This was another "two-act" with the boys adding characters to their plots by adding variations of their own voices. Glenn was the chuckling straight man, while Gene played the piano and was the voice of Jake—and Jake's girl friend, Lena.

Lena ran a boardinghouse of sorts, and Gene and Glenn were boarders. Jake was the handyman with a somewhat dimly lit mind, and—as was the wont of all comedy relief men—he was always getting into some sort of trouble. At one point in the plot he had proposed to Lena, and on his wedding day he was kidnapped. We forget why—or who would have wanted him—but kidnapped he was. Gene and Glenn had a tremendous national following.

Royal was especially sparked in his programming activity by the competition of radio's new arrival—William Paley and his Columbia network, which, Royal decided, was not going to be a flash in the pan. The competition that CBS afforded NBC made for some pretty wild and interesting maneuvering.

Bing Crosby had quit Paul Whiteman's Rhythm Boys and decided to become a single. The word back in New York was that it looked as if Crosby were going to make it with a new style of singing. Rudy Vallee had made a million with his nasal twang and saxophonic arrangements, but this Crosby had something new. A deep, deep voice— but not really a bass. It had resonance, all right, but it didn't have that formidable "Asleep in the Deep" quality.

It was nice, smooth—and sexy. They called it crooning. He took liberties with the lyrics, and sometimes didn't sing certain words at all—he just went "Boo, boo, boo, boo." Like Jolson, he whistled the bridge of a song occasionally.

Crosby was a pretty good-looking young chap—even though those ears stuck out a bit. But what interested the programmers at the network level was that voice.

Both NBC and CBS were interested in obtaining Crosby.

"In those days," Royal recalled, "we weren't paying anything to singers. I think Kate Smith was on sustaining—working for nothing because the exposure helped her personal appearances. Of course, at that time NBC had everything its own way. The CBS program lineup couldn't compare to ours, but little by little, Bill Paley was moving in. He got Morton Downey from us with money. The Boswell Sisters and the four Mills Brothers went over to Columbia, too. Then I heard he was after Crosby.

"Naturally, when two networks are after a guy he'd be a chump to take the first offer that came around. We both entered bids—and between us we got that pot pretty sweet.

"One day I walked into Deac Aylesworth's office and told him that Columbia had offered Crosby $1,500 a week for a quarter-hour sustainer Monday through Friday.

"Aylesworth told me to match it, but not to go any higher. Then Bill Paley threw in something that we couldn't—a screen test at Paramount. We didn't have an 'in' with any movie studio, and Paramount owned half of Columbia then. So we let him go.

"This was competition of the most elementary nature,

and it was good for broadcasting. I never resented Bill Paley's aggressiveness—I admired it."

Royal reveled in Paley's competitive tactics. So much so that as soon as he heard that Columbia got Crosby, he called in his assistant, Phil Carlin, and asked him: "What's the name of that pain-in-the-neck lawyer that I threw out of my office last week? The one who was trying to sell me a singer?"

Carlin had no trouble remembering the lawyer-agent's name.

"Well, look," Royal said. "I can't do this myself, because I told the guy not to come back here—but go find that singer. Tell him I've changed my mind, and I might be interested in putting him on the air after all. See if you can get him under contract. Watch the money, but don't tell him exactly what I have in mind."

Carlin couldn't tell the young singer what Royal had in mind because Royal didn't tell *him*.

Royal had heard that Crosby was booked on CBS to do fifteen minutes, five nights a week from 10:00 to 10:15, but that he had a head cold and wouldn't be able to start until about Thursday of the first week.

The NBC program chief decided to put the new boy in fifteen minutes ahead of the Crosby time—9:45, on Monday night. He didn't keep it a secret, either. NBC's press-relations people were told to get hot on the newcomer.

And so it was that Russ Columbo made his radio debut on NBC. This was the beginning of what the newspapers called the Columbo-Crosby feud. Actually, if there was a feud, it wasn't Crosby's or Columbo's at all. It was Royal's and Paley's.

Radio's Royalty

"I don't think Columbo had a chance," Royal says today. "But Crosby certainly got over his cold in a hurry; he was on his show that Monday night."

Remembering Columbo, we're inclined not to go along with Royal's guess that he wouldn't have made it in the shadow of Crosby's sensation. By the time of Columbo's accidental death while showing off his gun collection, Columbo was gaining well-deserved fame of his own. In fact, recalling the movie shorts he made with Crosby, the column items in the press about who was to become the "king of the crooners," Columbo probably would have scored big. There were only two of the "Crosby type" in those days. Later, came Perry Como, Frank Sinatra, Dick Haymes, *et al.*, and there seemed to be room for all of them . . . and the Elvis Presleys and the Frankie Avalons, too.

When John Royal talked about that competitive play between NBC and CBS, his eyes twinkled and he smiled the satisfied smile of a man who had enjoyed every minute of it.

"You know," he mused, "I often used to wish I had a percentage of Bill Paley's printing bill. This man *believed* in printed presentations. Everytime I turned around someone handed me a new, beautifully printed CBS brochure —and generally the duller the program, the more beautifully printed the presentation.

"One day somebody sent me the most elaborately printed book I'd *ever* seen. It was all embossed on expensive paper. It was an announcement that Columbia was to carry the *first* Shakespearean Festival in radio—starring Burgess Meredith. Well, this did it. If Paley hadn't used the word 'first,' I'd have just figured that these were the dog days and CBS was coming up with something to fill out the summer schedule and give the papers something to write about. But he used that word—*first*."

Royal said that NBC had been doing Shakespeare when he arrived on the scene. In fact, the network had tried it two or three times a week during the daytime. And it was, he said, "dull as dishwater." NBC had broadcast summer Shakespeare for three years—and now CBS comes along "with this *first stuff*."

Royal put in a phone call to John Swallow, NBC's program expert on the Pacific Coast.

"Where's Barrymore?" Royal wanted to know.

"Are you kidding? He's in the gutter," Swallow answered.

"Well, go find that gutter," Royal yelled, "and get in there with him and get him out of it! We're going to repel the English invasion! Burgess Meredith is going to do Shakespeare on CBS, and we're going to put Barrymore against him."

Swallow found Barrymore easily enough, and offered him a fat fee if he'd come back to New York and perform the Bard's works on NBC. Barrymore accepted but not instantly. There were a few little personal provisions he wanted. One—he had thought of a title he wanted the series to bear. "Streamlined Shakespeare." Royal said okay. Two—no one was to interfere with his personal comings and goings while he was in New York. Royal agreed again, so much so that after listening to many warnings about Barrymore's inability to cope with the bottle he called in a couple of NBC shopmen and had them build an iron pipe "fence."

It was a three-sided affair, waist-high and about two-

and-a-half feet wide. It resembled, if anything, a large baby-walker without wheels. The idea was that a man could walk into this iron contraption and, should he begin to fall, he could grip the little fence at any point and hang on. The man in the case being Barrymore.

The press made quite a lot of hay with this story—and there was much speculation as to whether John Barrymore would be able to stand upright all the way through a Shakespearean drama or not.

Even Royal became a little concerned. There was too much smoke not to expect a small blaze someplace.

"I called Swallow," Royal said, "and asked him if he would do the curtain speech—the introduction—on the first program, just in case. I told him that if Barrymore came through all right, he could have him do the openings on subsequent shows.

"By now the papers were full of the Barrymore-Meredith battle of Shakespeare. It was like a heavyweight championship. Naturally, I booked the show at nine o'clock on Thursday nights—exactly opposite Columbia's program."

Royal and other NBC brass sat in a listening room at NBC to hear what would happen on the first show. There was some nervous speculation among the executives.

Barrymore had picked *Hamlet* for his premiere performance.

"When Swallow started his introduction," Royal remembers, "I had a mild case of nerves. Nothing really serious—but there was that moment of doubt. Then Barrymore's rich voice filled the room.

"The war was over. Barrymore was sensational. This

was the kind of dramatic dynamite that made showmen weep with appreciation," Royal said.

* * *

Almost from the beginning the advertising agency began to play a large part in developing radio fare. The radio stations and networks were allowing the agencies the same 15 percent of the cost of time that newspapers and magazines offered in the cost of space when they placed a client's business—but in radio there were no illustrations to prepare, no type to order, no photographs to retouch—only commercials to write. So it was that the agencies moved into the area of program content in a big way. While the networks held the reins on deciding what kind of programs it would broadcast and when, the agencies were influential in that they held the purse strings and had everything to say about what was done with the manufacturer's broadcasting budget . . . and, more importantly, whether the manufacturer would even *have* a broadcasting budget. At the outset most of the money spent in radio advertising had to come from cash earmarked for other media—newspapers, billboards, and magazines.

Without going into complicated detail, the reason advertising agencies play such a great role in "running" the radio and television industry is that in the beginning poor, starving radio, unlike the wealthier press, did not have the financial wherewithal to make the agencies toe the mark. So it was that the advertiser wielded the big stick and decided on programs.

"Some agencies did the industry a great service," Royal said. "The J. Walter Thompson Company brought up a man named John Reber who opened up a whole new line of thought when he started a radio department at the agency. He hired writers and producers for shows—people with special talents and imagination to invent radio commercials for the agencies' clients.

"Lord & Thomas Company and J. Walter Thompson were the great advertising agency pioneers—and nearly all the big houses were soon to follow—McCann-Erickson, Young and Rubicam, Benton and Bowles—and scores of others.

"We had to put our foot down fairly often in those days. We still do so, sometimes, today in television—but the agency people are a little better educated now. In the old days they thought if they sponsored a show they owned us. The agencies wanted to hire and pay off their own engineers . . . they'd demand a studio for eight or nine hours when they really needed it only for three. Every time we'd tighten up our reigns at the network a little bit, they'd think we were trying to rob them of their 15 percent.

"Agencies were often very right in second-guessing what kind of programs the public would like. And they were awfully wrong sometimes, too. That was when the network got tough.

"I remember when Aylesworth opened a talent booking agency to make things a little easier. The advertising agencies raised all kinds of cane. They didn't want NBC to book talent—they wanted to do it. And they did it with a vigor and seriousness that often reminded you of the old cloak-and-dagger stories. They had suddenly found themselves in show business, and there was great competition for star talent. But this competition was good for radio.

It Sounds Impossible

The group that certainly had nothing to lose and everything to gain was the public—who got all this entertainment for nothing."

Among the agency-inspired fiascoes of which John Royal spoke was a little gem that Standard Brands tried out in all good faith in the Sunday night 8:00 to 9:00 P.M. spot on NBC that had been vacated by Eddie Cantor.

"This time period had done great things for Chase & Sanborn Coffee," Royal recalled, "and this particular time period had a great listening audience, we knew.

"Well, the J. Walter Thompson agency people had a great idea. They were going to uplift all America by presenting 'Operas in English.' The country wasn't quite ready for that after Eddie Cantor, and the show died on its feet. I told John Reiber, the agency radio director, what I thought of this turkey—and he yanked it off the air. Naturally, he needed not only a replacement but also something that would appeal to the great masses they were disappointing.

"Reber went after Major Bowes immediately. Bowes was doing an amateur show locally in New York on WHN.

"That's how 'Bowes' Amateur Hour' got booked. 'Operas in English' was so lousy."

In Royal's day NBC was actually two networks—the Red and the Blue. The NBC Red Network, with WEAF, New York, as its key station, was the *original* National Broadcasting Company. The Blue Network, using WJZ, Newark, as its flagship, was the "little brother" network. In many big cities NBC had two outlets—one Red the other Blue. The Red was the bigger of the two; consequently, it was the most sought after by sponsors. It offered more major cities, higher-powered stations, and a better sampling of the nation than the Blue.

Radio's Royalty

"Thank gosh for the Blue Network," Royal said. "The Blue Network saved NBC's life because this is where all the public-service programs went. And it wasn't a disposal operation, really, because these public-service features got full network treatment—they were really big time—and they reached a sizable audience."

Some years later the Federal Government was to find that the Red and Blue services of NBC were, in reality, two separate networks, and ordered RCA to divest itself of one of the networks. Naturally, it decided to keep the commercially profitable and larger Red service.

The Blue Network kept this rather intriguing name for a year or so until, under new, independent management, it became the American Broadcasting Company.

Who thought up the names for the Red and Blue networks? And why were they called Red and Blue as opposed to One and Two, or Colossal and Stupendous, or Damon and Pythias? we asked Royal.

"Nobody thought up these names at all," Royal said. "Like everything else in their day—Red and Blue just happened. In the beginning of networks you didn't have automatic switching or little buttons you pushed to control the system. Each of the wires that fed the stations had a plug and a hole on the main switchboard. Now, there were a lot of holes and a mess of plugs, and if you got the wrong plugs in the wrong holes, you were in trouble; you'd have the right station get the wrong programs.

"So when the telephone company first started sending radio programs down wires, NBC was called the "Red Network" because the plugs were painted red. Later on, when the secondary network came into being, those plugs were painted blue. That was the Blue Network."

Simple?

CHAPTER 9

Meanwhile,
Back in Blighty

BECAUSE there will always be an England, certain broadcasting jargon will be ever theirs and will cause many an untutored American to wince when he first hears it.

If a chap sees a *loosebox*—he's looking at an open space in a printed schedule.

A *compère* is a Bert Parks—an emcee.

Now, if you have an OB—it has nothing to do with a baby doctor. It means, simply, *Outside Broadcast*. British radio terminology is really much simpler than American. Over here we call OB's *nemos*. At least, we used to. Now we call them *remotes*.

Tops and tails—easy. The written openings and closing of shows. In America they're known as *intros* and *outros*.

And the systems differ in more ways than terminology and slang. The difference in American and European radio goes back to the beginnings of broadcasting.

Meanwhile, Back in Blighty

Actually the brainchild of European inventors, radio was not doing nearly so well in Europe as it was in the United States in the first days of the twenties. There was one good reason for that. America was ripe and ready for radio. The postwar boom, a daring change in outlook, manners, and morals had made most Americans tremendously curious as well as very active. Prohibition helped push the excitement along, strangely enough. The bottle ban became a real challenge to Americans seeking pleasure. It became smart to drink from a flask, smart to drive a car, and smart to own a radio. These things, coupled with a bit of prosperity, made the twenties roar in America.

Great Britain didn't experience a roaring twenties.

There was no great postwar boom; unemployment was high; and England was totally exhausted from the four long, tough war years.

Britain procrastinated in the field of broadcasting, but as the English public read of America's rapid advances in radio the hand of British authority was forced—authority, meaning the British Post Office, which controlled and operated the telephone, telegraph—equivalent to our Western Union—all forms of wireless operation. This was a nationalized government monopoly.

The American pattern of broadcasting had considerable impact on the development of the British system in the beginning, though in time the two were to be completely different. The BBC—yet to be—was based on a concept of public service, while broadcasting in the United States was fully integrated into the business system.

An English ban imposed on amateur broadcasting was not lifted until late in 1919. The Marconi Company began

to broadcast on an experimental basis from Chelmsford—
the same year that KDKA made its debut in Pittsburgh.

Late that year, the Post Office withdrew permission for
these broadcasts because of interference with "reception
tests" being conducted by the Department.

On February 14, 1922, the first regular broadcasting
service was started from a little village with the improbable but completely English name of Writtle. The Writtle
station, also operated by the Marconi Company, was interested both in technical developments and in programs.

Staffed by bright and ebullient young men, the Writtle
station was mostly fun and games. Headed by P. P. Eckersley, a bubbly, talented extrovert, the programs were
mostly brilliant improvisations.

Writtle once broadcast a night of opera, provided by
Eckersley alone. He not only sang the arias but also made
his own commentary.

The spirit of the station in Writtle is best exemplified
in its theme song, which was sung, of course, by Eckersley
—in a high tenor voice, accompanied by a battered and
tinny-sounding piano:

> Dearest, the concert's ended,
> And wails the heterodyne,
> You must switch off your valves,
> I must soon switch off mine.
> Write back and say you heard me,
> Your hookup, and where and how.
> Quick, for the engine's failing,
> Good-bye, you old low-browe!

Two other firms, Metropolitan Vickers and Western
Electric, each with American connections, were anxious

to compete with Marconi. Soon they were operating experimental stations in Manchester and London. Other applications for permission to broadcast flooded the Post Office—twenty in two months.

The reply was always the same: "The ether is full."

Jarred into action, the Post Office, in a typically civilservice maneuver, asked the manufacturers to get together themselves and decide what they wanted to do. They were asked to prepare a cooperative broadcasting scheme, or, at the very most, two schemes for consideration by the Post Office authorities.

The manufacturers named a committee of six major companies to devise a plan. After months of haggling among themselves, and bickering with the Post Office, the British Broadcasting Company, Ltd., was formed late in 1922.

This was a business enterprise, underwritten by manufacturers, to provide a broadcasting service to the country. It was to be supported by a tax of ten shillings on set owners, and, by Post Office ruling, its dividends were limited to $7\frac{1}{2}$ percent.

Four years later, through constitutional arrangements, the company became a corporation, and the BBC, operating with a Crown charter, came into existence.

Then, through luck, fate, or perhaps predestination—the man involved was a devout Presbyterian—an event occurred that changed the future of broadcasting not only in Great Britain but also in the world.

One dreary, rainy October day in 1922, a young Scotsman who'd been job hunting for six months scanned the advertising of public appointments in *The Times* of London—known here as help-wanted ads:

It Sounds Impossible

> The British Broadcasting Company (in formation). Applications are invited for the following officers: General Manager, Director of Programmes, Chief Engineer. Only applicants having first class qualifications need apply.

The Scot wrote an application and posted it in the letter box of the Cavendish Club. Nearly two months later he got a reply and was interviewed several times. On December 14, 1922, he was appointed General Manager of the British Broadcasting Company.

He was J. C. W. Reith, a thirty-four-year-old engineer who hated "smooth-running jobs," and who, in the spring of 1922, had resigned an executive post in a Coatbridge engineering firm.

Reith had a good war record. He was wounded in action. He had spent nearly a year in America supervising and expediting the production of munitions for the British.

Reith obviously was a man of character and firm convictions, yet why he was selected for the job still remains a mystery. Perhaps his employers were as confused as Reith, who, in his diary, wrote that on the day he got the job, "I did not know what broadcasting was."

But he soon found out. This stern, devout man set his stamp on broadcasting in Great Britain—and in Europe.

In his autobiography, Reith wrote:

So the responsibility, as at the outset conceived, and despite all discouragements pursued, was to carry into the greatest number of homes everything that was best in every department of human knowledge, endeavor and achievement and to avoid what was or might be harmful.

Meanwhile, Back in Blighty

Although he was later accused of giving the public not what it wanted but what the BBC thought it should have, the true answer was that few people knew what they wanted. And fewer yet at the BBC seemed to know what they needed. But, the BBC reasoned, it was better to overestimate than to underestimate.

When Reith took office, the BBC staff numbered four. A year later, it had grown to 552, and Reith and his colleagues, despite much criticism in both Parliament and the press, instilled their values in broadcasting. The wireless to them was an instrument of public good, not a means of pandering to the wants of the people. Broadcasting should be elevating, and not debasing—like the cinema.

Fortunately for Reith, he had the complete backing of his board of directors. And certainly this man was a demon for work—sixteen hours a day, seven days a week. Reith at last had found the job he "wanted." He loved it.

In Reith's own words on his philosophy of broadcasting:

It was in fact, the combination of public service motive, sense of moral obligation, assured finance and the brute force of monopoly which enabled the BBC to make of broadcasting what no other country in the world has made of it.

Without the brute force of monopoly we might still have said many of the things that were said in those early stirring years. That broadcasting was a potential influence, national and international of the highest import. That it would have been a prostitution of its worth had the service been used solely for entertainment in the narrow sense. That the informative and educational possibilities must be recognized and developed. That sooner or later broadcasting would cross all paths and be recognized for what it was. That all and sundry without let or hindrance, might enjoy the interests and diversions hitherto reserved for those with the twin keys of fortune—leisure—money. There would be no house, however favored, into which some new interests and pleasures might not be introduced.

But without monopoly, many things might not have been so easily done that were done. The Christian religion and the Sabbath might not have had the place and protection they had, the place and the protection which was right to give them. Sabbath—"one day in the week clear of jazz and vanity and such like; an effort to preserve the inestimable benefit of a day different from other days."

In 1927 the government bought out the set manufacturers and formed the BBC—a public-service corporation acting under a Crown charter. The charter is renewable by Parliament every ten years. The corporation is a self-supporting agency. This is important in understanding this system. Each set owner in Britain is taxed one pound, and these funds are enough to operate the three domestic services of the BBC. The BBC does *not* depend on annual appropriation from Parliament. It is a part of the British Post Office.

The BBC is run by a director general who is named by a nonpartisan board of governors which is appointed by Parliament.

The BBC has three national program services: The Home, The Light, and The Third Programme. The Home and the Light are national networks, and operate very much like CBS or NBC. The Third Programme is a unique experiment in broadcasting. It is a service broadcast from 6:00 P.M. until midnight, and it breaks away from many of the conventional concepts of programming.

For example, complete plays are often broadcast, and run two and a half hours on the air. The first act might be done from 7:00 to 8:00 P.M., and then an hour of dinner music, followed by the second and third acts, ending at about 10:30 P.M. The traditional time segments—fifteen minutes and half-hour—as we know them—have been tossed out the window. One program may run forty-eight minutes, the next an hour and twelve minutes.

Besides the three national networks, radio in Britain is decentralized on a regional basis. There is the Scottish Region with studios in Glasgow and Edinburgh; the Welsh Region with studios in Cardiff; the North Region with offices in Manchester and Newcastle; the West Region in Bristol and Plymouth; and Northern Ireland with headquarters in Belfast. Each of these regions has a writing and production staff, and can break away from one of the national networks and present local programs that are suitable for its own listeners on its own wavelength. For example, the Welsh Region broadcasts a number of programs daily in the Welsh language, and the Scots, who are highly nationalistic, originate a number of their own shows.

The system works very well, and there is little, if any, interference with BBC operations, policy, or programs by the political party in power.

A New York radio executive recently said all radio outside America is dull and lifeless as dishwater.

A chairman of the BBC said American radio is a hodge-podge of vulgar advertisements, jingles, and hot jazz.

Both views are absurd, of course.

Let's examine the good and bad points of these systems.

The BBC likes to be known as a public-service corporation. Yet the BBC does not play so great a part in the daily lives of the average family as American radio. The BBC will probably deny this, and point with pride to its school broadcasts, its news and news features, excellent talks and discussions, and really fine documentaries. Quite true, and in many cases these programs are superb radio.

But you'll listen in vain in the morning on the BBC for such simple public-service items as time signals, weather, news every hour, special farm programs, road information, best "buys" at the market, shopping services, or listing of free entertainment.

Under the BBC system, there are no *local* radio stations. The BBC does a limited amount of regional broadcasting in Scotland, Wales, and the Midlands; but great cities like London, Manchester, and Liverpool have no radio service of their own. There's no radio forum to debate local issues, no place for local candidates to speak, no local news or features, no radio aid to the Boy Scouts, Y.M.C.A., or similar organizations in their annual fundraising campaigns.

This is a radio service we casually take for granted in any city or town in all sections of the United States. In most large cities, there is broadcasting service twenty-four hours a day. Not so in Britain.

Sam Slate joined the New York office of the BBC in 1945. His suite was in the International Building on Fifth Avenue. The program staff he headed was a mixture of English, Canadians, Australians, and Americans.

The "international problem" Sam faced was complicated slightly by the fact that he was from Georgia—southern accent and all.

Sam's recollections of his BBC days give one pause:

*   *   *

The New York office had many functions. There were resident BBC correspondents in Washington and at the

Meanwhile, Back in Blighty

United Nations whose daily news programs were fed to London via these studios. BBC had a direct line into the master control of both NBC and CBS, and the right to record and broadcast news and public-service broadcasts of interest overseas. Presidential speeches and major events, such as the opening of Congress or the United Nations, were handled in this way.

The BBC had three exchange programs which were broadcast simultaneously here and in England: "Atlantic Spotlight" on NBC, with Leslie Mitchell in London and Ben Grauer in New York introducing top talent from both sides of the Atlantic; "Trans-Atlantic Call" on CBS, a serious documentary reporting on all aspects of British and American life; and "Trans-Atlantic Quiz" on ABC, a team of experts in London and New York trying to find out who knew the most about the others' country.

The American team consisted of Christopher Morley and John Mason Brown; the British, professor D. W. Brogan and Joyce Grenfell, the actress. The questions were extremely difficult, and Brogan and Morley's knowledge was amazing.

The New York office negotiated script and music rights, arranged for American visitors like Bob Hope and Jack Benny to appear on the BBC in London, and constantly produced short pieces of program material for the many BBC programs.

A special on the American Indian of the West once requested a greeting in Sioux to all British schoolchildren. London was tactfully told that the nearest Sioux Indian was 2,500 miles from New York and that it would take three days and cost several hundred pounds to produce one. The offer was refused with the tart observation that America was just too bloody big. BBC producers never considered the size of the United States, and were irritated when it was called to their attention.

I remember once vacationing in western North Carolina, and getting a London phone call asking me to drive over to New Orleans for lunch and cover a jazz concert. I patiently explained that New Orleans was a good two-day drive and that I couldn't get there in time. My London colleague said: "All right, old boy, if you don't want to cooperate, just say so. . . . Sorry I upset your holiday." And he rang off. A year later in London I wangled an apology by taking him to the Royal Automobile Club, the equivalent of our AAA, and proving the mileage.

Of course, words were an even greater problem than distance. Once, producing a profile of Governor Eugene Talmadge of Georgia, the phrase "popping his red suspenders" slipped through. An amusing but quite inaccurate picture for our British audience, for there "a suspender holds up your socks, and braces, old boy, your pants."

Another program, on tobacco cultivation, went into detail on the type of dirt required and its preparation. Soil would have been correct, for dirt is trash or filth, the kind of stuff you sweep from your sidewalk—no, I really mean pavement.

And once, in the sacred cloisters of Broadcasting House, London, I shocked a score of colleagues of mixed sexes by apologizing for being tardy because a virulent carbuncle on my "fanny" had required medical attention. Later I was tactfully told that in London "fanny" was a sexual organ. Much better to have said "on your ass, old boy, but then you Americans just don't know."

William A. Reid, North American Director for the

Meanwhile, Back in Blighty

BBC, my boss, was one of the finest men I've ever known. He was an American's idea of the typical Englishman: portly, pipe-smoking, liking his sherry and port, traveled, completely honest, and given to blunt, direct answers and observations. One evening, after discussing problems over a pleasant dinner, we returned to the BBC studios.

Because BBC's overseas service was the equivalent of our Voice of America, we daily recorded talks in many languages, and air-expressed them to Bush House, London, using female engineers.

We discovered a rather pretty, pert young girl engineer in a very intimate embrace—with another young lady. To say that I was surprised would be a bit of British understatement.

Reid puffed his pipe for a second, and then, without raising his voice, said, "Young lady such conduct will not be tolerated on the premises of the Corporation."

I don't really understand the English but I sure as hell like most of them.

CHAPTER 10

The Lord
for Lord's Sake

AS JOE COOK remembers . . .

*   *   *

It would be about 20 below, and the snow would be so icy it would crunch under your boots, and the night would be so still that you could hear a kid whistle all the way from Belknap and Banks clear over to Twenty-first and Tower. That's what the nights were like in Superior, Wisconsin, when we got our first table-model Crosley. And those were the nights I liked best because my dad would generally invite a few folks over to listen to something on the radio. Not everybody in Superior had radios in 1930. Only a few on our block. The Carters had a floor model with a loudspeaker that was separate. It had a cutout of a ship on the grillwork of the speaker, and my buddy Don Carter and I used to watch it and pretend that the voices were coming from that ship. And if you looked and listened long enough, it got kind of spooky.

But those winter nights in the thirties were great . . . and Sunday night was the best. My mother served a little

The Lord for Lord's Sake

something like sponge cake or sandwiches. Generally the visitors were the same people—but very interesting to an eight-year-old boy who belonged to people who had a Crosley table-model radio. There would be Captain Dermody of the Salvation Army, and Mrs. Dermody. And Ernest Willoughby who lived over on Oakes Avenue, who had actually built a radio, and Belle, his wife. The reason Sunday nights were best was Seth Parker.

My dad would look at his railroad watch after all the small talk was done, and he'd say, "Well, it's Seth Parker time." He would walk ceremoniously to the radio and turn it on. "It'll warm up in two shakes of a lamb's tail," he'd announce.

While he was doing that, my mother would assemble the living-room and dining-room chairs in a semicircle in front of the table-model radio.

When the radio started to hum, my dad would consult his watch again and say, "They'll be giving the time signal pretty soon." The voices or music from our local station, WEBC, would fill the room, and everybody would smile, and start to talk at once.

Then my dad would say, "Shush," and every man in the room who owned a watch would bring it out and stare at it.

"Here is the *correct* Central Standard time from Bagley and Company—jewelers at 315 West Superior Street in downtown Duluth," said the voice from the radio. "At the chime . . . 10:00 P.M. exactly!"

Chime!

"Well, they're a half a minute slow," my dad would say.

Then it would happen. Seth Parker and his Jonesport

"neighbors" would come on the air. The highlight of the hometown American Sunday night. There were the hymns —and between the hymns a loosely woven story concerning the neighbors of Jonesport. The format of the program had the neighbors meeting at the Parkers' house—just as they were at the Cooks'—to sing hymns. We learned from the dialogue about their ups and downs, their engagements and marriages, their little frustrations—which, I guess, were just like ours. The depression was on, and the talk sounded good—and encouraging. And the hymns— oh, how sweet!

There was always a little prayer, generally led by Seth himself—and then it was over . . . and my mother served the sponge cake.

Seth Parker was a man named Phillips H. Lord who was to parlay religion and crime into well over a million dollars.

Phil Lord was the first successful independent producer in radio. That is, he sold the entire show as a package to NBC. For a flat fee he delivered everything to them. He made several unique contributions to dramas and documentaries. He was first a great showman, but he was also a great salesman.

Phillips H. Lord came to New York in 1927. He was the son of a minister, a graduate of Bowdoin College, had taught school for two years, and wanted to write. He tried, with no success.

One evening, at the home of a friend, he listened to a radio broadcast of rural life. It seemed so exaggerated and untrue that he jumped into a taxi and rushed to the broadcasting station to tell the performers how to make the sketch realistic. Naturally, they ignored him, but his insistence won him a trial on the air. And Seth Parker was born.

This was Lord's story, and whether it's true or not doesn't really matter. His idea was right, and almost overnight he was a national figure.

In addition to the Sunday-night Seth Parker program, which had a regular audience of four million, Lord wrote books, magazine articles, and songs. He made phonograph records, and went to Hollywood to star in a movie called *Way Back Home*. He made a continental tour with his Seth Parker singers. They "sang along" thirty years before anyone ever heard of Mitch Miller.

In 1931, after a Washington benefit and a private meeting with President Herbert Hoover, Lord was presented to Congress as "the source of more cheer and contentment and wholesome enjoyment than any other person living in the United States today." The members of the House of Representatives rose to their feet, and applauded.

A devout disciple once wrote a very long poem called "When Seth Parker's on the Air." Lord liked to quote it on client calls or when he was trying to impress people, which was all the time. One stanza will give you the general idea:

A sort of wholesome atmosphere's lingering round this hour,
As pure as morning dew that falls upon the fragrant flower.
These gospel songs bring memories that haunt each sweet
   refrain,
Refreshing as the summer breeze that cools the coast of
   Maine.
And when the neighbors "gither" and "Ma" Parker strikes
   the chord,

It Sounds Impossible

Somehow I feel I'm getting better acquainted with the Lord.
The dear old hymns my mother loved I learned so long ago,
Just stir the embers of the past into a brighter glow.
Of all the hours I listen to, there's none found anywhere
So quaint and wholesome like as when Seth Parker's on
  the air.

At the peak of his success in 1936, Lord suddenly decided to take a cruise around the world in a sailing ship. He chartered a three-masted schooner, christened her *The Seth Parker,* and embarked from New York bound for the South Pacific via the Panama Canal.

Lord underwrote most of the costs of this strange venture by persuading Frigidaire to sponsor a series of broadcasts from *The Seth Parker.* The programs were not an unqualified success.

The Seth Parker cruised leisurely down the Atlantic coast, anchoring at Baltimore, Charleston, and Savannah for broadcasts. The parties after the programs were not exactly the type one expected from a radio personality who proclaimed, "Just have faith in God, and by His grace you'll reach the Promised Land." The press notices were critical.

"I've been asked a million times why I left my work and started on such a trip," Lord was quoted as saying. "I did it because I loved the sea and because I wanted to see the world.

"Although we failed in our original purpose, the journey—we got as far as Samoa—was by far the greatest adventure of my life, and if I had the chance I would repeat it.

"As I look back on it, I realize that *The Seth Parker* was dogged by Lady Bad Luck."

The Lord for Lord's Sake

Although $200,000 was spent in renovating the vessel, she did not prove seaworthy, so Lord was "somewhat apprehensive" when they were overtaken by a tropical hurricane in February, en route from Tahiti to Samoa.

"After a hurried consultation with the skipper, Captain Constantine Flink, formerly a navigator in the Imperial Russian Navy, sent out a radio request for information, asking the position of the nearest ships," Lord said.

"H.M.S. *Australia,* with the Duke of Gloucester aboard en route to Panama, altered its course 70 miles and went to *The Seth Parker.* By this time the storm had subsided and it was thought that our schooner could make Samoa, 300 miles away, without help.

"Five hours later a second hurricane hit *The Seth Parker,* already badly lashed by the first storm. This time an SOS was sent out, and the *Australia* doubled back on its course to *The Seth Parker.* The rescuing vessel took nine men, leaving Captain Flink, two sailors and myself."

But the nation's press was suggesting that it might be a publicity stunt—and so were government officials of other countries.

Phil returned to New York in 1937, not only broke but discredited in the industry. Yet, in a short time, he was peaking again with two very successful radio programs.

He produced and sold commercially a half-hour dramatic program based on the exploits of the G-men, using material from the files of the FBI. Although "G-Men" was an instant hit, the program lasted only twenty-six weeks. It foundered on a very strong personality conflict between Lord and J. Edgar Hoover.

Phil converted the series to "Gangbusters," which played for years on both radio and TV, and he obtained his material from police files throughout the country. His method of operation was simplicity itself.

He'd pay a small fee for a five-hundred-word outline of famous police cases in various parts of the United States. A vast majority of this material came from police reporters who'd covered the story and were delighted to pick up a few extra dollars. On rare occasions he got stories direct from police officials or publicity-seeking district attorneys.

This research was converted into half-hour dramatic scripts for $200 by any of a score of free-lance writers. It was formula stuff, and crackled with action, sound effects of machine guns and police sirens. About the only problem then facing the writer was to devise a new method for the cops to crack the cases. A vast majority of crimes are solved by stool pigeons tipping the police or by sheer dumb luck. Thus, "Gangbusters" became a happy mixture, half hokum and half fact. Deductive reasoning is really the province of fictional characters like Nero Wolfe, Perry Mason, or Sherlock Holmes.

Next came "We the People," based on the premise that almost everybody has one interesting story or fascinating experience worth repeating. Lord employed several researchers who clipped newspapers and magazines for the unusual, the odd, the bizarre, the absurd . . . and this was given to a producer. He phoned the persons in question, talked with them at length, and if they seemed interesting and articulate, invited them, all expenses paid but no fees, to New York to appear on "We the People."

Though handicapped by the network ruling against prerecordings, "We the People," with an inspired title, was an instant success. Often, though, the amateurs would give a fine performance in rehearsal, and go haywire during the broadcast. It would be standard procedure today to pretape such a program.

At the peak of his crime-fighting career, Lord decided to revive Seth Parker. He sold the idea to the Vick Chemical Company to promote the use of Vick's Vaporub. Somehow, runny noses and chest congestion were not congenial with "Hymns My Mother Loved" and Sunday-night prayer, and the series was junked—this time forever. In rapid succession came the famous "Mr. District Attorney" series; "Sky Blazers," the dramatization of the lives of famous pilots; "Woman in Love," a soap opera; and scores of other projects ranging from Gangbuster sweatshirts to Seth Parker baked beans.

By 1938 The Phillips H. Lord organization of some thirty people occupied the twenty-fourth floor at 501 Madison Avenue, with Phil's office and its adjacent terrace more elaborate than any Hollywood set. Here Slate spent two weird and wonderful years doing publicity, exploitations, research, writing, producing, casting, and even arranging parties.

* * *

Phil was in his late thirties, and a handsome man: brown hair, ruddy complexion, trim, neatly dressed, the mere suggestion of a dimple, a quick smile over very white teeth, sharp features, nervously energetic, but also arrogant, unpredictable, and quick-tempered. A great salesman. Phil seldom read a book, went to a play or a movie, or listened to the radio. He was amazingly ignorant of the world and its problems.

Phil had sublime confidence in his ability to do anything. He once asked me to call on several Broadway producers and offer his services as a consultant for $1,000 a week on new plays. Yet he had never written or produced a play, or appeared on Broadway. He was quite sincere about his new project, and very upset when there were no takers.

Lord spent his summers on his island off the coast of Maine or on his boat. One hot, humid August day he appeared in the office, bronzed, smiling, exuding health, and called a staff meeting.

"You know," he said, "I don't want you to think I've just been doing nothing but fishing and swimming and having fun. That isn't true. The old Lord mind"—he had a disconcerting habit of referring to himself in the third person at times—"never rests. In the last few weeks I've dreamed up two new ideas for radio programs. One is terrific, it's wonderful, it can't miss. It's a typical Phil Lord idea. The kind of program that everyone expects from radio's Number One idea man. The other is not quite so exciting, but it will make good listenable radio. It's about the kind of idea that the *average* man would have."

A writer snickered. He was promptly fired, and the meeting adjourned.

Lord had one very dramatic story that he always reserved for important visitors or magazine feature writers. It was known around the office as "De Lord's double cross."

After explaining in some detail the fate of *The Seth Parker,* and that he had been flat broke, literally, on the beach on a South Sea island, Phil would walk slowly around his enormous office and recite:

"I was walking along the beach one night, moody, despondent, thinking of the futility of life, and the welcome release of the grave. The pounding surf beat a sad tattoo. I stumbled along, blindly, without purpose or direction, ready to fling myself into the breakers.

"Suddenly I heard the motor of a small plane. I was near the edge of a landing field. A giant floodlight was turned on the runway. Beyond the field its glare spotlighted the white cross of a tiny church. I could almost hear the sound of all those wonderful old hymns I learned at the knee of my dear old mother. Instantly, almost miraculously, I was happy, glad to be alive, the master of my fate once more. I knelt on the white sands of the beach, and gave thanks to God and asked for aid and comfort. God heard my voice, and I came to New York and with His blessing achieved all this.

"Now I'd like to show my deep appreciation to God in some tangible form. Of course, I realize that Seth Parker brings solace and peace to millions, and my other shows give great, relaxing entertainment, but I'd like to feel I've made some permanent contribution.

"I've decided to rent, in perpetuity, the top of a tall building overlooking Central Park. There I will erect a huge white cross and bathe it in soft lights every evening. Perhaps it will help some poor sinner like myself and bring courage and hope to the weary and despondent in this great city as it did to me in the islands that gloomy night a long time ago."

An energetic real-estate salesman, after reading this story, called Lord to rent him the ideal site for his cross. The reply he got from Phil did not bring him comfort or solace.

It's true that Phil was an expert in phony emotionalism, corny characters and drama. Also, Phil was fortunate in living after Marconi, for radio paid, and paid well, for such talents in those days. In an earlier era Phil would have been a smash hit as a medicine man with cooch dancers and snake charmers selling Lord's Magic Elixir to cure everything.

Yet, for better or worse, Phil Lord changed the patterns of the radio programming in the decade before the war. Seth Parker was the forerunner of scores of dramas and soap operas based on the simple lives of simple people. "Gangbusters" and "Mr. District Attorney" were partially responsible for the flood of "who-done-its" and cops-and-robber dramas on both radio and television. "We the People" underscored the vast quantity of program material available in correctly using real people instead of actors.

"Besides, it's much cheaper," Phil always said.

But Phil did not change with the times, and now sits on his Maine island, probably wondering about today's broadcasting, definitely not satisfied with being just a listener.

CHAPTER 11

The Dawn
of the Golden Age

HERBERT CLARK HOOVER of Iowa had been inaugurated as the Thirty-first President of the United States, and Richard Evelyn Byrd flew over the South Pole. Charles Augustus Lindbergh married Anne Spencer Morrow, and Ernest Hemingway had just written *A Farewell to Arms*.

On Broadway, *Journey's End* was playing to standing room only at the Henry Miller Theatre, and *Strictly Dishonorable* was at the Avon.

Maurice Chevalier and Jeanette MacDonald were starring in a movie called *The Innocents of Paris*, and Mary Pickford was in a flicker called *Coquette*.

It was the era of *Variety*'s famous headline, "Wall Street Lays an Egg," reporting the stock-market crash on October 29th when over sixteen million shares changed hands on a single day.

It Sounds Impossible

NBC put the opera *Aïda* on the air over a network of forty-five stations.

Radio was going big time, and the men who introduced the programs—the announcers—were gaining a fame all their own.

There were Niles T. Granlund, who identified himself on the air as N.T.G.; Graham McNamee, Phillips Carlin, Ted Husing, Milton Cross, Norman Brokenshire, and Jimmy Wallington.

As John Royal pointed out earlier, these men became idols in their way. Women loved the maleness of their voices. Men admired their diction and their "command of the English language." Radio listeners began to accept these intonations as regular sounds in the home. These bodyless voices sent imaginations soaring, and rumor had it that a top announcer got paid by the word, or the second, or the minute—which was really not far from wrong—although an announcer at a radio station generally worked a full day for a salary that was nothing astronomical. As the depression set in, a station announcer's pay ranged anywhere from $15 to $50 a week.

Of course, the big-timers on the networks who were in demand for the top dramatic and variety shows were part of the new "star system" in radio, and generally were in a bargaining position. A varsity announcer could command several hundred dollars a week on the right shows.

Today it is not uncommon for a New York announcer to gross from $50,000 to $100,000 a year by virtue of the "talent fee" policy employed by most big stations, networks, and independent producers of programs and commercials.

Among the great "old guard" of big-time announcers, still very active on a national level, is Jimmy Wallington.

The Dawn of the Golden Age

There was a time—the time of the beginning of the Golden Age of broadcasting—when Wallington seemed to be everywhere. What jobs Wallington didn't have, Norman Brokenshire, Graham McNamee, or Milton Cross did.

Jimmy was the slim, suave, sophisticated NBC announcer of "The Chase & Sanborn Hour" with Eddie Cantor, "The Fleischmann's Yeast Hour" with Rudy Vallee, and "Town Hall Tonight" with Fred Allen.

Wallington—to lesser announcers—was the *voice,* and Wallington was the *fashion plate.* "I played it to the hilt in those days," he said. "I wouldn't think of being seen after six o'clock without a tux. For the big nighttime shows we wore tails."

In going over the files of stacks of pictures of announcers in the early thirties it seems that everybody had to look like Wallington. Moustache, slick black hair, perfect posture, dressed to the teeth. Along with building what is now called an "image," Jimmy also did a great job of announcing. He was an avid student of words and sounds. He did comedy sketches with Eddie Cantor long before anyone thought of hiring actors and stooges for radio comics.

Jimmy lunched with us at Louis and Armand in New York. He's a little heavier today, perhaps, but there's still the moustache—and something new, an ever-present, expensive cigar. The voice is possibly even more resonant than it was in the thirties—a great voice indeed.

Wallington is not likely to forget the early thirties. His name was as well known as any movie star's, and his voice was infinitely better known.

His career began in 1928 when he went to WGY in Schenectady, where his job was—oddly enough—developing makeup for television. General Electric had been experimenting in the medium. Only a year before, AT&T successfully sent a recognizable picture with sound from Washington to New York, and in 1928 Jimmy figured that television was just around the corner. He was one of the first television performers of all time. The shows were experimental in nature, and sending devices used the scanning-disc method. "Electronic" TV was a long way off. Because Wallington was also fascinated by WGY's shortwave operation, he used to ask the station officials to put him on shortwave a great deal.

When KDKA and WGY were fighting it out for radio "firsts," WGY conceived the idea of sending some shortwave programs to the Byrd Expedition in Little America. The families of the members of Byrd's expedition were invited to send WGY letters to be read on the air to their loved ones at the South Pole. In those days it was the only contact that Byrd's men had with the folks at home. Young Wallington became the chief letter reader on these Saturday-night programs. Between letters he would introduce little entertainment features.

"After reading these letters for a year and a half, I had an inside knowledge of the members of the expedition that was unique," Jimmy said. "But what to do with this knowledge was the question."

Wallington wasn't long in finding an answer.

"The chief announcer at NBC in New York was a fellow named Curt Peterson. I knew he was a singer and rather proud of it. Inasmuch as I was hiring for the weekly General Electric musical program, I thought it might be a good idea to invite Mr. Peterson up to Schenectady to sing for us. He accepted—and I assigned myself to do the announcing on that particular program.

The Dawn of the Golden Age

"Somehow we got talking about my experience with the Byrd Expedition. Then Curt said the magic words. He suggested I might like to come to New York and meet the Byrd Expedition when it arrived in New York Harbor. I was overjoyed.

"This was a dream come true," Jimmy remembers. "I was getting out of the small town into the big city."

It was March of 1930 when Jimmy arrived in New York; but because the Byrd men didn't arrive until June, the neophyte NBC staffer got in quite a few licks on the air before his first special event.

His coverage of Byrd's arrival cinched him as a prospect for the big time.

"They had two ships. One was the *Eleanor Bolling,* an old converted whaler, and the other was *The City of New York.* I was sent out in a seagoing tug called *The Relief.*

"It was five o'clock in the morning when we met the Byrd ships 350 miles out at sea. They handed me a megaphone, and I called over to *The City of New York* and asked if Commander Byrd was aboard. They said Yes —and then a voice came over the water:

" 'Isn't that Jimmy Wallington?'

"Well, I was pretty thrilled. It was the voice of Commander Byrd. He had recognized my voice calling across the waves even though he had never heard it closer than nine thousand miles away on radio. I transferred to *The City of New York* and came into New York Harbor with the men. It was the most thrilling day of my life up to then—and it was the wedge that opened a career in broadcasting for me."

It was entirely an ad lib broadcast. Graham McNamee was on the U.S.S. *Macon,* sharing the word picture with

Wallington. The two announcers followed the entourage all the way to Albany where Governor Roosevelt presented Commander Byrd with a medal.

It was the first of many such shows covering major events.

Soon afterward Jimmy Wallington found himself assigned to the biggest shows on the air. He grew a moustache so that he would look older.

It was while Jimmy was announcing the Rudy Vallee Hour for Standard Brands that Eddie Cantor came into his life and made him a national institution of sorts.

Vallee had taken an unknown violinist by the name of Rubinoff under his wing, and made up an audition package called "Dave Rubinoff and His Orchestra." The members of the NBC music staff made up the aggregation. Inasmuch as Fleischmann's Yeast—Rudy's sponsor—and Chase & Sanborn Coffee were both products of Standard Brands, the company had a proprietary interest in Vallee and his ideas. Wallington announced that audition.

"They liked Rubinoff and his violin, and the orchestra was fine. Maurice Chevalier was signed to star, and the show was launched on NBC. Chevalier returned to France after twenty-six weeks, and Eddie Cantor took over. This was the program that became the famous Eddie Cantor Hour on Sunday nights," Jimmy said.

Cantor was the biggest draw on Broadway at the time— and was the first comedian to have his own weekly show on network radio and the first to use an announcer as a straight man.

There was no one on the program except Cantor, Wallington, and the Rubinoff orchestra. Jimmy and Eddie did all the parts.

The Dawn of the Golden Age

"We even played the women's roles," Jimmy said. "Eddie would be Edwina and I would be Jeanette. We'd be in a laundry or at a card party. Gad, I wonder if I'd even want to hear a playback of those sketches today. But they did get laughs."

There were no radio stooges at that time, and no one had thought of using actors to augment the comedian's material.

"We'd play Englishmen or Dutchmen . . . anything the script called for. It was great experience. Later on, as the show expanded, we took additional characters—some of them became famous in their own right. There were Parkyakarkus and Bert Gordon, the Mad Russian. So many great people."

The Eddie Cantor we remembered on the air generally "went serious" for a minute just before each program's sign-off. We wondered whether this was a "good guy" act or whether Cantor was sincere about it all—so we asked about the Cantor of the 1930's.

"The Eddie Cantor I knew was a very humble individual," Wallington told us. "This isn't what most people think of Eddie Cantor as being. I can honestly say that, having worked with him for twenty-six years, off and on, I've never had an argument with him. He would always listen. He realized, perhaps, that I knew a little more about radio than he did in the early days . . . although he certainly knew more about show business than I'll ever know—or anyone will ever know. But when it came to approaching a microphone or getting an effect, Cantor would ask. He was a great boss."

In 1935 Jimmy's wife, Anita, was captain of the Rockettes at the Roxy Theatre, and when the Radio City Music

Hall opened, the famous long line of girls moved, with Anita at their helm. Then, suddenly, she became desperately ill and was taken to St. Mary's Hospital in Brooklyn.

Jimmy was told that her days were numbered—but Anita never knew.

"I had to go to Philadelphia one day to work a show at the Poor Richard Club with Lowell Thomas," Jimmy told us. "When I got back to Anita's hospital room, she said: 'I had a visitor today, Jimmy. Mr. Cantor came over for a while'."

Jimmy asked her what she and Eddie had talked about.

"Let me ask you a question, Anita," Eddie had said. "After you get out of here, what's the first thing you want to do?"

"Well, if it's still playing at the Music Hall," Anita had replied, "I'd like to see *Roberta*. I've heard so much about it. I understand Fred Astaire and Ginger Rogers are just wonderful as a team."

"Yes," Cantor had replied, "it's a dancer's picture, all right. It's truly a great show. I hope you get to see it."

With that, Cantor left the room.

"That was a Friday afternoon," Jimmy recalled. "On the following Tuesday morning a movie sound truck pulled up in front of St. Mary's hospital with a print of *Roberta* and a sound projector—the big one—such as they use in the theaters. They moved all this gear into Anita's room, and she saw *Roberta* on the ceiling over her bed. The picture was still playing at the Music Hall. It was her last motion picture. She died two weeks later.

"It was a side of Eddie Cantor I'll never forget," Jimmy said.

The Dawn of the Golden Age

There are a couple of little sidelights of Wallington's announcing career that were signs of the coming times in broadcasting. He weathered the ill-fated "Operas in English" and was the voice that introduced Major Bowes' Original Amateur Hour to the NBC network audience. Wallington was there for many important premieres in radio.

He remembered meeting Ed Wynn the night after Ed started his series as the Fire Chief for Texaco. Wynn was guesting on the Rudy Vallee program that night from the New Amsterdam Roof. Wynn said: "You know, Jimmy, it's a very funny thing. For twenty years I've been building myself and billing myself as the Perfect Fool. And in one night—on the radio—I am no longer the Perfect Fool. I am the Fire Chief. I reached more people in that one broadcast than I did in my twenty years on the stage before this."

Wallington's still very much around. There hasn't been a week since 1928 when he hasn't been on the air doing something. His current commercials include Seven-Up, Nu-Soft, General Electric Refrigerators, Du Pont, Sea Mist, and Bit-O'-Honey candy bars, to name a few. The ebullient, laughing curlyhaired wonders of today's television will have to work terribly hard to make their audiences feel as safe, secure, and genuinely entertained as Jimmy did when he was—as he puts it—doing shows.

Humor and music were the mainstay of the big radio variety show. America couldn't get enough of it. The radio comedian was the country's new hero.

The format became fairly well standardized. There would be the comic himself, his announcer, the orchestra leader, a vocalist or a group, and three or four assorted stooges. This became the comedian's "family." No one was spared the barbs of his humor.

The "stooge" system worked exceedingly well. Listeners began to wait for some of the actors on comedy shows with as great an anticipation as they did for the star. Many carved lucrative careers for themselves in the characters they created on a comedian's program.

From Fibber McGee and Molly came "The Great Gildersleeve." Jerry Colonna became a national figure because of the Bob Hope show. Jack Benny's "Rochester" —Eddie Anderson—has done a great deal of work on the stage, screen, and television without the master—and for handsome stipends, too.

Along with the popular stooges came the guest stars.

The Rudy Vallee hour was the first big showcase for extra added attractions—well known and unknown. It was Rudy Vallee who first presented Edgar Bergen and Charlie McCarthy to radio audiences. Alice Faye made her debut with Vallee.

One of his early guests was a young comic who had done some funny things in the stage version of *Roberta*— Bob Hope.

In 1932 a juggler by the name of John F. Sullivan left vaudeville for radio and, over the years, became not only a tremendous favorite with the public, but the radio comedian's radio comedian. He called himself Fred Allen.

Here, too, was the "family" formula. On the program were Fred, his wife, Portland Hoffa; his announcer, Jimmy Wallington; his orchestra leader, Peter Van Steeden; his singer, Kenny Baker; and the ever-present sidekicks Minerva Pious and Sam Levine. Later was to come a great weekly adventure in comedy on his show—a trip down "Allen's Alley" to meet the incomparable Ajax Cassidy, Senator Claghorn, and the irrepressible Mrs. Nussbaum.

Allen wasn't an instant hit on radio. There was something going against him that could be fatal in broadcasting. He had a terrible voice. Because of the poor quality of the loudspeakers of the early thirties, Allen's voice often had the effect of scraping a set of fingernails across a blackboard. But the public began to overlook his shortcomings in resonance for his superiority in comedy.

For the most part, Allen wrote his own stuff. He was the master of the sharp barb and biting satire. He sometimes built a simple joke into an entire sketch. When the king-sized cigarette was introduced, Allen devoted nearly a whole show to it.

He was always "the leader" in his relationship to the people on the show. Another mark of the Allen format.

Here was a rather typical Allen opening from twenty years ago:

WALLINGTON: At this time of year, ladies and gentlemen, the sun shines, the birds sing, flowers bloom, and the sap is running from the trees. And speaking of sap—that reminds me. Here he is now—Fred Allen, in person!

ALLEN: Thank you, thank you. And good evening, ladies and gentlemen. And before we start, Mr. Wallington, fun is fun. But I resent that "sap" innuendo.

WALLINGTON: But, Fred—

ALLEN: Some day you'll overdo it with one of your introductions.

WALLINGTON: But, gee, Fred. You only gave me one line. It's the only chance I have to let people hear the real Wallington. I let myself go.

It Sounds Impossible

ALLEN: One of these nights you'll let yourself go, and find that I have beaten you to it. I once had another announcer who let himself go during the introduction. Do you know what happened to him?

WALLINGTON: What?

ALLEN: He is now announcing in the Cromwell Drug Store at Forty-fourth Street. If you should go into that particular drug store and order ham and eggs, the gentleman who takes your order will turn toward the kitchen and shout, "Ham 'n' eggs!" And then from somewhere in the back, another voice echoes, "Ham 'n' eggs!" And then, from way back in the dark, dingy confines of this drug store—a lone voice will cry out, "Coming up!" That is the announcer who once worked for me and once, only once, mind you, let himself go during my introduction. Now what do you say?

WALLINGTON: If that guy's getting three square meals a day, he's better off than I am.

ALLEN: You are undernourished with that rotunda under your vest? Your stomach looks like either end of the Staten Island Ferry. If you open that coat, you will probably hear a watermelon calling its mate!

WALLINGTON: Oh, yeah?

Along with the family relationship of characters on comedy shows, stars sought out running gags and devices of association. Cantor started the whole thing with constant references to his five daughters and his wife, Ida.

Jimmy Durante capitalized on the size of his nose, and on every show called a great deal of attention to his "schnozzola."

Bob Hope used the nose device, too. Gags about his ski-snoot drew lots of laughs on the old Hope radio show.

Fibber McGee delighted millions with his closet. On

nearly every show he brought down the house by opening the mythical closet door, and—with listeners building their own mental picture of what was stored there—there was the tremendous crash of paraphernalia. There would be a pause, then the final tinkle of a small bell as it hit the floor. Another laugh, then another short pause, and McGee uttering the words that never failed to get applause: "Gotta straighten out that closet one of these days, Molly!"

Jack Benny's Maxwell, his sub-basement vault, his violin, and his stingy ways all carried over to television. His devices were sound and durable. Benny brought another comedy formula to radio. He was seldom content with telling a gag and letting it alone. A great Benny device is to top the gag and then come back again and top the topper.

At one time in the era of his radio show, Benny, according to the script, had a polar bear named Carmichael. Rochester, his valet, was scared to death of the animal, and refused to go into the basement where Benny kept it. In one show Rochester insisted that Carmichael had eaten the gas man. Benny kept telling him that he was being silly. But Rochester persisted. During another program the doorbell rang, and Rochester answered it.

"Who is it, Rochester?" Benny asked.

"It's the gas man!" Rochester replied.

"You see?" yelled Benny. "You see? It *is* the gas man. I *told* you Carmichael didn't eat him. (PAUSE) What does he want?"

"He wants to know where the *other* gas man is!"

Then came the feuds.

These little battles between air personalities proved

to be very good for grabbing newspaper space and giving the gossip columnists something to talk about. Walter Winchell and Ben Bernie had one of the first really publicized feuds. It began on the air with Winchell doubting Bernie's musical ability. The columnist claimed that the famous bandleader couldn't even play the violin he held when he conducted the orchestra. The friendly barbs carried over into the movies when producers realized that having both Winchell and Bernie on the same screen would increase box-office receipts.

Jack Benny and Fred Allen began their feuding with Allen sprinkling his script with jokes that started "Why, Jack Benny is so cheap, that . . . ," while Benny referred to Allen's face as being a picklepuss.

Bob Hope and Bing Crosby conducted the most famous of the latterday feuds, with Hope everlastingly needling Crosby about his age and his diminishing hairline, while Crosby took picks on Hope's nose and broadening girth.

The late W. C. Fields used the feud technique with tremendous success with Edgar Bergen's dummy, Charlie McCarthy.

"Is that your nose, Mr. Fields? Or is it some kind of a flamethrower?" Charlie would ask.

"Ho, ho, ho . . . ," Fields would reply. "You'd better come out of the sun before you come unglued."

Fields would turn on Charlie with barbs like, "Quiet, you termite's flophouse!"

Or Fields might start out charmingly with: "Hello, Charles, my little friend. I was thinking about you only yesterday."

"You were, Mr. Fields?" Charlie would exclaim.

"Yaas, I was," Fields would answer. "I was cleaning out the woodshed at the time. Reminded me of you."

The Dawn of the Golden Age

For eight years, starting in 1930, a tall, unhandsome, unlikely man named Raymond Knight held forth on a peculiar and very funny program called "The Cuckoo Hour." It was an important contribution in that it was the first comedy show designed especially and exclusively for radio. Knight's material wasn't a retread of vaudeville, movie, or nightclub material. He found his satire all about him—within the hallowed halls of NBC. The program was a national institution to millions. The show was sometimes sponsored, sometimes sustaining. For a while it ran a half-hour, and at other times, fifteen minutes.

Ray Knight was probably the most talented broadcast comedy writer ever to come along. His technique was simple. He slipped a blank piece of paper into a typewriter and started writing. He wrote about anything—the day's headlines, the weather, women's fashions, department stores, banks, or bagels. He never owned a gag file—so, as he used to put it, "I'd get a topic and just go."

On "The Cuckoo Hour," Knight called himself Ambrose J. Weems—the Voice of the Diaphragm.

A typical "Cuckoo Hour" might start with the announcer saying, "Good evening, friends—and what of it? The next half-hour is to be devoted to a broadcast of 'The Cuckoo Hour,' radio's oldest network comedy program, and if you think that isn't something—maybe you're right. Station KUKU features Ambrose J. Weems and other disreputable things which are too numerous to mention at this time. Are you still with us? Ho hum. Well, there's no accounting for tastes."

He'd then introduce Knight, who in turn would set the theme, if any, for the show, and introduce his unlikely partners in crime such as Mr. Bernelli, a theatrical gentleman, and Mr. Twilling, a businessman who wants to become a theatrical gentleman, and therefore a logical mark for Mr. Bernelli, who was really a con man. Then there was Mrs. Pennyfeather. She was the first parody of radio's own performers—a takeoff on broadcasting's home economist or lady lecturer. Among her suggestions on baby care, for instance, was a toupee for baby's little bald head so he wouldn't catch cold. In the script she demonstrates with a baby who, during her lecture, grabs Mrs. Pennyfeather's hair. In Knight's funny mind it turns out that Mrs. Pennyfeather, too, is bald, and the gurgling kid pulls off her wig . . . known in those days as a transformation.

It was enough to keep any family home on any given evening—even though you could buy a ticket to the local movie house for a quarter. The depression was on, and a dime could buy enough popcorn to sate the family until morning. This entertainment was free.

CHAPTER 12

Accent on Agony

A g o n y on the air was a natural development in the mid-thirties—probably because there was so much of it around. In April of 1935 Congress voted an economic relief program involving about five billion dollars, and the Works Progress Administration was born along with the Social Security Act.

Roosevelt was having an uphill fight with the Supreme Court. His National Recovery Act was declared unconstitutional.

Millions were on relief, and the welfare dole was gigantic.

The economics of the country caused considerable trouble in the business of matrimony. Despite the tremendous output of love songs on the radio, fewer couples were taking the Big Step, and most of those who did soon ended up fighting about money—of which there was precious little.

Needless to say, the lack of lucre to buy The Necessities of Life caused some fairly testy moments in the best adjusted households. A henpecked husband of the thirties, whose earnings left something to be desired, might even resort to taking a nip from the now legal bottle . . . and just when he could least afford it. Further nagged by a complaining wife, he might resort to smoking cigarettes or occasionally staying away from home overnight doing Heavens knows what. In tears, the wife might scream some very mean things at him as he came dragging his weary bones home after a night of Forgetting the Depression. The next step was obvious. If she yelled enough, he might just give her a fat lip and slam out of the house for good.

In this atmosphere of economic tension in the household there appeared a cabdriver from the Bronx named Lester Kroll.

Lester Kroll was to find that domestic unhappiness can be an economic boon under the right auspices. A harried housewife could be worth a million. But not at first.

When he was twenty-three years old, this thin, almost gaunt, dark-haired young man married a tall, pretty college girl named Stella Lang. Shortly afterward he began driving a cab. He wore a fur coat and a chauffeur's cap and was considered a good cabbie. But even good cabbies didn't make a lot of money.

Three years after he took the taxi-driving job, Stella began action for a legal separation. She claimed he wasn't supporting her and their two boys. According to the records, Stella claimed that Lester told her he was making only $11 a week. The Court listened to her, and ordered Lester to pay Stella $20 a week. When he tried to prove he couldn't, Court lowered the amount to $5 a week. But Lester didn't believe in alimony, apparently, and was sent off to jail for nonpayment. He served one term of three months—to be followed later by another, shorter term. Once the arrears on Lester's alimony got as high as $1,200. He was twice cited for contempt of court for not paying up.

It might be hard for this situation to be thought of as a springboard to great fame and wealth for Lester Kroll—but it was, and Lester was to show what can happen to a man facing nagging misfortune in an America where there is commercial radio.

While in jail, he organized the Alimony League among his fellow prisoners. He was later to make this league a very active one, with a lobby in Albany to help beat down some of New York State's archaic and ridiculous alimony laws.

What powered Lester into the great economic dream of the 1930's was his desire to be a playwright.

He quit driving a cab and picked up a picket sign which he toted down to the WPA Building. There he marched for days. His cause: That the Works Progress Administration add more talent to the Federal Writers Union and give more aspiring authors a break.

He had been writing plays under the pen name of Jack Anthony, but found no market for unsolicited works by unknown authors in those days of depression.

Somehow, he worked his way into the WPA project that was dedicated to various literary, musical, theatrical, and artistic projects—sometimes to the dismay of the WPA laborer who was taking a lot of comical guff from people about his leaning on his shovel. The WPA was intent on building culture along with bridges and play pools in parks.

It Sounds Impossible

While a part of the WPA, Lester learned about radio. This was for him. By now he had two assets in experience —a bad marriage and the knowledge of how broadcasting is done. He must have reasoned, also, that you didn't have to have a successful marriage to give advice, or be a seasoned broadcaster to broadcast.

He established The Marital Relations Institute in New York City, and opened it to any and all married couples with domestic difficulties. While smarting over the failure of his first marriage, and suffering defeat at the hands of the courts, he had studied psychology and divorce laws until he had worked up a "patter" of truisms and truths. He charged five dollars per visit.

Lester engaged in public speaking around the New York City area, and could often be found giving free lectures in the flea-circus belt around Times Square.

In April of 1932 he went on the air over a small station on Long Island, WMRJ, in a series titled "Talks by John J. Anthony—Dedicated to Helping the Sufferers from an Antiquated and Outmoded Domestic Relations Code." By May he had discarded his script—and never used one again after that.

Simultaneously, on New York's WMCA, another show had built a big audience. It was called "A. L. Alexander's Court of Good Will," and its format consisted of local lawyers and judges giving legal advice over the air to listeners who wrote in with problems.

Alexander's listeners could be counted by the millions. This was one of the greatest services ever offered on radio. And it was free. Too much so. Suddenly, the New York Appellate Division barred judges and lawyers from giving legal advice over the air. The show was immediately canceled.

Accent on Agony

Lester Kroll—now John J. Anthony, Expert in Marital Relations—picked up his agent, Manny Swars, hightailed it over to the studios of WMCA, and offered himself as a replacement. He made capital of the fact that he was the Director of the "famous" Marital Institute, and a "seasoned" broadcaster. He reasoned that the two qualifications combined should add up to a smash show.

There is no record of WMCA's reaction to the five-foot six-and-a-half-inch Broadway type with the steely eyes, the well-trimmed moustache, and the slick manner—only that he was signed for $50 a week to replace Alexander and the lawyers on a trial basis.

"Mr. Anthony" was off and running.

Never was a program concept uglier—or a show more fun to listen to than "The Original Good Will Hour." Fifteen to twenty people on a Sunday evening would appear before Mr. Anthony's microphone and eat their hearts out over who did what to whom at home. Agony-loving New Yorkers ate it up.

The show was built in a very simple way. Listeners would write to Mr. Anthony and tell him about their troubles. He then would screen out about thirty-five of the most dramatic—but not *too* dramatic—and invite these people to his broadcast. It was often suggested in the press that the people who wept into his microphone were paid actors and actresses. This was never so. There is a section of humanity that loves to broadcast its troubles—anonymously or otherwise, it makes no difference.

A few years ago, when NBC assigned Joe Cook and Helen Hall, roving reporter for *Monitor,* to do a series of remotes from Home Term Court, a real domestic-relations court in New York, they thought their biggest problem might be to get witnesses to sign statements of permission for their remarks to be used on the air. Not one person in twenty cases refused. They wanted to be heard . . . names or no names.

But Mr. Anthony used no names. He used initials— and not the initials of the person being interviewed or "heard." Some of the interviewers insisted that Anthony tell them which initials would be theirs so they could call home and be sure the kids would know which one was Mama.

Before each broadcast Mr. Anthony would call into a studio all those who were ready to tell their stories on the air. At this session he gave them a little briefing—no names, no addresses, don't mention religion, speak up, don't be afraid, don't touch the microphone, please be vivid, but not too vivid.

"If your husband beats you," Anthony might say, "just say he beats you. Whether he beats you with a pipe or a bullwhip is not important. It is important that he beats you."

Sex was ever present, but generally unspecified. A listener with an imagination to match his curiosity could have a field day listening to Anthony draw out his confiders on the air.

At each program's opening, Anthony's announcer, Roland Winters, who later starred in many films and on Broadway, stepped to the microphone, and in a most cultured, resonant, dramatic voice, said:

"You have a friend and adviser in John J. Anthony. And thousands are happier and more successful today *because* of John J. Anthony!"

Anthony's paycheck rose with his agonizing star. After a while his show was heard simultaneously on two New

York stations; then he went network. *True Story* sponsored "The Original Good Will Hour" for a time, and Anthony's income went from $50 to $500 a week, then to $750. His consultation services went from $5 a visit to $25. At his peak, his earnings reportedly totaled $3,000 weekly.

One show-business barometer that indicates the popularity of a program is the degree to which it is parodied on other shows, and how many jokes comedians make about it. John J. Anthony became a household word. Old gags were built around the "confession situation"—and somewhere in the joke was the line, ". . . so what is your problem, madam?"

Anthony did some good, too. He took his cases and his people seriously, and had real compassion for them. A case picked at random from the thousands he aired went like this:

A paralyzed Brooklyn woman who hadn't been out of the house for eighteen years yearned for fresh air, the grass and the trees, and when it seemed impossible she wanted to die. Her plight was broadcast, and thousands responded with donations. A special ramp was built so she could be moved outdoors, and Anthony helped her start a lending library to pass the time and give her an interest in life.

We found one of the few quotes John J. Anthony gave to the press in a New York *Post* of February, 1944:

"I have interested more people than any man in America. First, I teach people what marriage is, and then give them a method of solving their difficulties. There is no formula, but I know if they will practice the Golden Rule, everything will be all right," Anthony said.

It Sounds Impossible

"The Original Good Will Hour" set a pattern for pain and poverty on the air that was to make a great deal of money for other producers who were to follow.

Latterday tours into the vale of tears included Jack Bailey's "Queen for a Day" ("My dear, just dry those tears now and let's see you smile. . . .") and Tommy Bartlett's "Welcome Travelers." Les Lear, who produced the Bartlett show from the Hotel Sherman in Chicago, was quite candid about the people "Welcome Travelers" helped.

"A good tear-filled interview is fine human interest—particularly when the case has good association with the listener, but we never fed on it. We liked to have some laughs, too."

Tommy Bartlett was probably the most able and least offensive emcee in the area of agony. He let the guest do most of the talking, and never goaded the interviewee to make the details juicier.

Lear and Bartlett tried hard to give their interviewees things they needed. If a woman on "Welcome Travelers" needed a wheelchair, she got one—probably motor-driven. If a kid was stranded in Chicago, he was most likely flown back to his home first class.

The woes of the plain people also made Walt Framer a big name in national radio and television. Framer had produced shows for a local station in Pittsburgh before coming to New York and bringing the country such programs as "Ladies Be Seated" and "Break the Bank."

Questions and answers for prizes was an established radio entertainment form when Framer created "Strike It Rich." Here, the popular quiz format was tied to human interest . . . mainly heartache. "Strike It Rich" featured real stories about real people who needed help.

Accent on Agony

Max Wylie, the advertising agency producer who was assigned to the program, described "Strike It Rich" as "a show in which we meet people in trouble and we witness the conquest of courage over despair."

A contestant on "Strike It Rich" would tell emcee Warren Hull why he needed a specific amount of money. Reasons ran the gamut—Braille books for a blind boy, a stove for a poor housewife's kitchen, a warm coat for a husband, a hearing aid for a mother.

First, the prospective contestant wrote to "Strike It Rich" where the truth of his need was carefully verified. On the program itself, the contestant answered five questions. He was give $15—provided by the sponsor. He could lose the $15 or he could win from $5 to $480—which was rounded off to an even $500 by the benevolent bankroller. Thus, three very dramatic elements came into play—conflict, suspense, and sympathy.

If a poor, needy soul bet his $15 and lost it on the quiz—other gimmicks were added to prevent the stunned contestant from leaping into the orchestra pit.

The Heart Line came to the rescue. A big red heart was set up on the stage. It lighted up whenever the producer pushed a button. A phone bell would ring, and Emcee Hull would pick up a disconnected phone and listen to Producer Framer tell the audience, through a filter mike, that a call had come from someone at home offering the contestant various gifts. These items might be the clothing the contestant was trying to win, money for the hospital, a place to live, a stove, or a car.

Then, too, many listeners and viewers sent money to the program to be put into a "Heart Fund" to be given to needy people at the discretion of the producers.

It Sounds Impossible

There was still another gimmick—the Helping Hand. People who were physically unable to make the trip to New York to appear on the show could write a letter and ask for someone to appear for them. As the letters came in, they were checked out for validity and okayed for broadcast. Then a Helping Hand was sought—generally someone famous. A letter was picked at random, and the celebrity appeared on the show to answer questions on behalf of the letterwriter.

But first the celebrity told a heartwarming little story of his own—of how he, too, was once down on his luck and needed, and got, a helping hand . . . and how it was just about time he passed along that good deed and tried to help somebody else.

Broadway and movie stars made very good Helping Hands, but the boxers, golfers, and ballplayers were the best. They had the best "down spots."

On the show the celebrity would cross his fingers, bite his lip, and grimace in agony as the questions were asked, in the fervent hope that he could answer them all correctly and earn the needed money for the person for whom he was playing.

He usually could.

We ran into a former associate director of "Strike It Rich" the other day, and we talked about some of the cases with him.

"I worked the show for six weeks," he said, "and finally I asked CBS to take me off it. My stomach began to bother me. Really. The last case I remember was one in which a family of five—Mama, Papa, and three beautiful kids appeared on the show. Mother was in a wheelchair. She had been paralyzed before she was married but bore 'The

Mister' three lovely daughters. Now she had just found out she had a terminal case of cancer. Papa wanted to 'Strike It Rich' to buy a little used car so he could take Mother around the country on a sightseeing tour before she died. Mother smiled through the quiz. They got the money for the car—and I retired quietly and became violently ill. I couldn't work 'Strike It Rich' after that.''

The poor souls who appeared on the agony shows and bared their misfortunes for the world to hear would have been wonderful students of the Stanislavsky School of Drama.

They knew how to suffer.

The Little Things
They Said

O N A N Y morning, the kids going to school, the men delivering the coal, the clerks behind the counters, the brokers at the stock exchange were reciting the lines the comics used the night before:

"Ya' wanna buy a duck?"

"Howdee, Bub . . ."

"I'm a ba-a-ad boy!"

"Say good night, Gracie!"

"That's my boy who said that!"

"Hello, Mr. Benny, this is Rochester!"

"That's pretty good, Johnny. But that ain't the way I heerd it. The way I heerd it was—one fella says to the other fella'—'Saa-aay,' he says—"

"Soooo-o-o-o!"

The Little Things They Said

"Duffy's Tavern where the elite meet to eat, Archie the manager speakin'—Duffy ain't here. Oh, hello, Duffy!"

"I dood it!"

These little catchphrases belonged to, in order of their appearance, Joe Penner, Titus Moody of Allen's Alley, Lou Costello, George Burns, Jimmy Durante, Rochester, the Old Timer on "Fibber McGee and Molly," Ed Wynn, Ed Gardner as Archie the manager of "Duffy's Tavern," and Red Skelton.

There were scores more. They became such a part of the American language that when General James Doolittle's men bombed Tokyo near the end of World War II, a Los Angeles newspaper headlined the story in a banner across page one that read:

DOOLITTLE DOOD IT!

These one-liners were an American phenomenon. They were the passwords of a brotherhood of radio-set owners—a fraternity of people with similar tastes—a horde of humor lovers who felt a kinship to one another when they bandied these lines about.

Jack Pearl as Baron Munchausen had the first big success with the redundant gag line. His weekly characterization was fashioned after the fabled Baron who was the world's greatest liar.

Pearl's straight man was Cliff Hall, a most competent actor who played the Baron's friend "Charlie." Pearl used a German dialect in the Baron's role, and each week the roof caved in when the two would get to the part of a script that went something like this:

BARON: Zo—I climbed in der balloon, und I vent over a 150 miles straight up in der air!

It Sounds Impossible

HALL: Baron, you could go 150 miles straight up in the air!! That's impossible!

At this point the Baron would chuckle and then pause:

BARON: Voss you *der*, Sharlie?

This was the big laugh.

HALL: No. I wasn't there. . . .

BARON: *Zooo* . . . I climbed in dis balloon, und . . .

Another big laugh.

Then, too, in the early thirties youngsters and adults alike started whistling, humming, and singing a new type of lyric. Along with such popular lyrics of the day as "Let's Put Out the Lights and Go to Sleep" and "Shuffle Off to Buffalo," new words were creeping into the average American's bathroom repertoire. Nonlove words like:

"Happy little motor, putt, putt, putt . . ."

"Twelve full ounces, that's a lot . . ."

"Bar-ba-sol, Bar-ba-sol!"

The first singing commercials were a great novelty, of course, and caught on immediately. Every new creation was sung from coast to coast. Ford came along with:

> See your Ford dealer, the price is low!
> And, baby, can those V-8's go. . . .

Pepsi-Cola did a tremendous job with their large economy pitch that went:

> Pepsi-Cola hits the spot!
> Twelve full ounces, that's a lot,
> Twice as much for a nickel, too . . .

The rush was on. Advertisers and their agencies suddenly went into the music business. Hometown stations composed their own jingles for local advertisers.

The Little Things They Said

Among national advertisers the commercials became more complex and heavily arranged, until today you find a typical big-time musical commercial made up of a seventeen-piece orchestra, a vocal sextet, and two soloists. The music is often written by a composer of the caliber of a Jerry Adler or a Frank Loesser. Adler has composed musical tributes to York imperial-size cigarettes and Kent-with-the-micronite-filter, to name just two. Loesser lent White Owl cigars the title tune from his Broadway hit *Most Happy Fella* for commercial purposes, and in another deal he let the Ford Motor Company have another song from the same show—"Standin' on the Corner" ("watchin' all the Fords, watchin' all the Fords, watchin' all the Fords go by!").

In latterday distillation some of the musical approaches to sales messages were not only popular; they were even slightly educational.

Time magazine gave the first critical review to a singing commercial when it cited United Fruit Company's pitch for bananas as being an outstanding piece of entertainment, education, and merchandising. A female character named Chiquita Banana—actually a lovely young lady named Elsa Miranda—sang about the proper care of bananas to a Latin American rhythm. It ended:

> Bananas like the climate of
> The very, very tropical equator,
> So you should never put bananas
> In the refrigerator.
> No, no, no, no!

Musical spot announcements can hit the nation with the impact of a smash-hit song out of Tin Pan Alley. Chiquita Banana is a good example. After the jingle became established on the air, columnists and comedians had a field day with banana jokes. For instance:

"I'm so mad I could put my bananas in the refrigerator!"

Naturally, the agency and the client feel this is the ultimate in broadcast advertising—to make the product a household word. In the rush to be musical and clever on the air, some advertisers allowed their agencies to create inferior jingles which actually became a deterrent to product sales. They annoyed the public because they were not well written, were unmusical, and often just silly. Their constant repetition on the air drove prospective customers away from the merchandise.

Occasionally, a very simple device would capture the public. In the early forties Cresta Blanca wines came up with a radio signature that was commercial simplicity itself—the spelling of the name of the product. Announcer Frank Gallop, at the end of the Cresta Blanca commercial, would recite the letters of the name to music—generally a background of strings playing pizzicato—his voice running uphill on the first word and downhill on the second:

(UP) C-R-E-S-T-A
(DOWN) B-L-A-N-C-A
(LOW) Cresta!
(HIGH) Blanca!
(LEVEL) Cresta Blanca!
(ORCH: *Plunk-plunk, plunk-plunk*.)

The extent of the success of such a commercial is pointed up to some degree by the fact that this announcement is virtually impossible to set down in type.

And radio gave America the "theme song."

Musical program introductions are still used in broadcasting, but not in the big way they were in the thirties. In those days, a theme song *said* something. It had thirty-two bars and a full-blown lyric. And they were beautiful. Any radio fan could sing them for you.

The kid shows came along with theme songs with a moral and a sales message of sorts. At 5:45 of any weekday evening in a home with children, everything stopped, including play, schoolwork, and supper. It was Little Orphan Annie time.

This was the story carried over from the comic strip, but with a whole new "family." There was Annie, of course— dauntless, fearless, kind, good-hearted, wise little Annie. Her "adopted" family consisted of Mr. and Mrs. Silo—see, they were farmers.

And then there was that good-natured, freckle-faced, happy-go-lucky, and not-so-smart-as-Annie kid down the road—Joe Corntassle. Joe sure was stuck on Annie, all right. But he never even kissed her.

Everybody's good friend and "uncle image" was Pierre Andre—the announcer. Nobody quite remembers if Pierre Andre sang that theme song or not, but the whole version opened every show:

> Who's that little chatterbox?
> The one with curly auburn locks?
> Whom do you see?
> It's Little Orphan Annie!
> She and Sandy make a pair,
> They never seem to have a care!
> Cute little she,
> That Little Orphan Annie!
> Bright eyes, cheeks a rosy glow,
> There's a store of healthiness handy,
> Mitze size, always on the go—

It Sounds Impossible

> And if you want to know,
> "Arf!" says Sandy.
> Always wears a sunny smile,
> Now, wouldn't it be worth your while,
> If you could be
> Like Little Orphan Annie?

Nobody ever said so, but we all imagined that the reason Annie was so great was that she drank her sponsor's product—Ovaltine.

And if Annie's adventures zipping around the world to Africa, England, France, and just plain taking care of the everyday tragedies on the farm didn't point out how important it was to get a good night's sleep and eat plenty of the right kind of food, General Mills of Minneapolis came out with a kids' serial that would:

Jack Armstrong! Jack Armstrong! Jack Armstrong! Jack Armstrong—The a-a-a-all-American boy!

> Wave the flag for Hudson High, boys!
> Show them how we stand!
> Ever challenging, we champions,
> Known throughout the land!
>   (Ra, ra, boola, boola, boola, boola,
>   Boola, boola, boola, boo, ra, ra, ra!)
> Have you . . . tried Wheaties?
> For wheat is the best food of man!
> They're crispy and crunchy the whole year through.
> Jack Armstrong never tires of them
> And neither will you!
> So . . . just buy Wheaties.
> The best breakfast food in the land!

The kids got the message—and Wheaties became the breakfast of champions and boys and girls alike! All hail

The Little Things They Said

Knox-Reeves—which is not a college, but one of the smartest agencies in all the land.

The dance remote was a great blessing to adults during the depression. Record sales were off because there was no place in the average family budget for them. Cabarets and ballrooms were places where rich young men took rich young women, while the general populace lived the experiences vicariously by means of the radio. So young daters rolled up the rugs in the living rooms and the boys in bell-bottom trousers and young ladies with crooked hemlines danced to the music of the "Ol' Maestro" Ben Bernie, and Art Kassel and his "Kassels in the Air." There were the Coon-Saunders band out of Chicago, and Jan Garber—the idol of the airwaves.

Aspiring announcers on their first dance remotes waxed verbose with phrases such as:

"From the beautifully appointed Green Room of Maria Kramer's Hotel Edison just off Times Square in the heart of wonderful Manhattan, Mutual sends your way, coast-to-coast, the Music of Yesterday and Today—styled Blue Barron's way!"

They'd overdo it sometimes in their enthusiasm . . . hoping that somebody who *was* somebody would put them on an honest-to-goodness network commercial program. Generally they wrote their own copy—if they used copy—and if they didn't, it'd come out something like:

"And now here on the Vincent Lopez bandstand, Johnny Messner steps mikeward to ask the musical question—"Tea for Two."

With most big bands on remote radio, the leader did much of the speaking. He was the personality. His voice, along with the theme song, set the band apart from the ordinary.

It Sounds Impossible

Many a sentiment was stirred in the dim light of a living room about midnight when Ben Bernie's closing theme on the radio meant that pretty soon the folks would be home and it'd be time to break up the party.

It opened with a chime—and that mournful brass section. Bernie couldn't sing—so he talked:

> Au revoir. Pleasant dre-ams.
> Think of us . . . when requesting your themes.
> Until the next time when . . .
> Possibly you may all tune in again,
> Keep the Old Maestro always . . . in your schemes.
> Yowsah, yowsah, yowsah.
> Au revoir . . .
> This is Ben Bernie, ladies and gentlemen,
> And all the lads
> Wishing you a bit of pleasant dre-ams.
> May good luck—and happiness,
> ˙Success, good health, attend your schemes,
> And don't forget
> Should you ever send in your request-a
> Why, we'll sure try to do our best-a
> Yowsah!
> Au revoir, a fond cheerio, a bit of a tweet-tweet,
> God bless you . . . and
> Pleasant dre-ams!

New York, Chicago, Hollywood, Des Moines, and Oconomowoc were lonesome ol' towns—when Ben went away.

Blood and Fire
and Private Eyes

A TALL, distinguished-looking young man smiled as he eased his lanky, immaculately garbed frame casually to a microphone in Studio Seven at CBS. In the control room a suave, dark-haired director watched the second hand on the studio clock move to the straight-up position. The cast of actors in the studio were ready, but not particularly tense. To a casual observer it was difficult to imagine that this handful of charming people were intent on scaring the living daylights out of several million citizens.

On cue, a sound-effects man turned the knob of a huge, specially constructed but unoiled door. The creaks and squeaks were picked up by a carefully positioned microphone, and the engineer boosted the volume. The piercing squeak continued uninterrupted for several seconds. A pause: then the director pointed at the tall narrator. A deep, resonant, ominous voice filled the control room with tones that were quite chilling.

It Sounds Impossible

"Good evening, friends of the Inner Sanctum," he began. "This is Raymond, your host, welcoming you to another half-hour of gore galore. Come in, won't you? and sit down. No, not there . . . you'll sit on Ezekiel . . . and he wouldn't like that. Besides, you'd probably find him pretty cold. We've been keeping him on ice for about six months now. That noise? Oh, that's his teeth chattering. No, not because he's cold but because he just finished going over tonight's story and . . . well, I guess you could call him a scared stiff! (SPINE-CHILLING LAUGH)"

And so began another "Inner Sanctum Mystery."

The guiding light—or errie glow—of this half-hour study of blood and terror was a rather mild-mannered but very shrewd producer-director named Himan Brown who, during radio's golden days and nights, presented another weekly mystery story called "The Adventures of the Thin Man." We still see Hi occasionally around CBS or ABC or Rockefeller Center with a box of recording tape under his arm. There are still some Hi Brown properties about— even though today the energetic Mr. Brown need not depend on any income he can derive from broadcasting. A great show packager was Himan—but an even better businessman and investor.

Back in the late forties a writer offered an original script to Hi in which a jealous husband pumped about eight slugs into his unfaithful wife while her lover looked on. Brown rejected it for "Inner Sanctum" on the basis that there weren't enough bodies and far too little blood.

Listeners with mental faculties higher than the average eight-year-old must have realized that Inner Sanctum was really a parody of itself. Brown kidded the pants off horror with his tongue-in-cheek openings and closings, using the

Blood and Fire and Private Eyes

too blood-curdling voice of Raymond, the host. But he was kidding on the square, for the stories were, for the most part, ghastly. They were unnecessarily unlovely. The atmosphere that "Inner Sanctum" created was one of violence, shock and, most of all, tension. It was radio drama at its most commercial. There was only the most superficial interest in characterization, since there was no time for building real-life people. The heros were indestructible. They could be banged over the head any number of times, shot, stabbed, beaten up, or pushed into a river.

The idea was simply to frighten the listener.

However, in its heyday, fifty million Americans found Himan Brown's philosophy very pleasant and releasing. How much it added to the chronic anxiety of a developing child no one will ever know.

Crime stories on radio were probably no worse, but certainly not much better, than their latterday counterparts in television.

The American paradox of death and violence as "entertainment" is difficult to analyze; therefore writers of the crime story in both mediums enjoy a curious immunity to criticism—and, in most cases, only modest payment for their works.

But blood, fire, and private eyes were big in radio.

The half-hour crime program began with Phillips H. Lord's "G-Men," "Gangbusters," and "Mr. District Attorney."

Lord's approach was different from the rash of thrillers which were to come later. His premise was almost sanctimonious. Crime does not pay—underline *not*. The good guys were smart guys who always brought the criminal to justice and his proper fate.

It Sounds Impossible

This immediately presented some problems.

Scripters adapting real-life cases had to be constantly figuring out some way to make the cops bright. Any police officer will tell you that there's a great deal of dependence on informers, as well as just plain luck in solving crimes. This isn't bad. It's just that not every case is closed by crack, complex detective work. And, too, criminals are a pretty stupid sort, and do idiotic things.

"Gangbusters" was the dramatized version of actual police cases, and generally involved a call upon a leading police officer who told his story to a scripter for a small sum and was eulogized across the nation for his brilliant police work. Slate wrote many of them:

*   *   *

I was in an eastern city interviewing a detective who was credited with breaking up a counterfeit money ring which had been all over the papers.

We were sitting in a local bar having a few orange flips when I finally asked him:

"What's the real story?"

"You wanna know what really happened?"

"Sure."

"Well, what really happened was that I used to play poker a lot. I was crazy about poker. Some days I'd play poker far into the night—and a couple of times I was late for work. Sometimes even two days late for work. Well, the Chief didn't like this. He told me either I quit playing poker or I was through. He really bawled me out. Well, three days later—I was late again. I didn't crawl out of bed until about noon. I had to think up something to tell the Chief. Boy, was I worried! Because anything I told him he wouldn't believe. He'd just yell some more about my playing poker, and I knew that maybe this time he'd really fire me."

The detective took a long pull on his orange flip.

"On the way to work I saw a real seedy-looking character standing on the curb looking very suspicious. I hadn't seen him around town before, but he looked like a terrible guy. After all those years you can spot 'em. Now, you know that cops don't go around putting the arm on just anybody. This was definitely a criminal type. Of course, if he wasn't there's still nothing to prevent me from giving this guy the onceover. And this guy was seedy. I'd hauled in a hundred of 'em.

"So I took him in. The Chief would know I was working.

"Imagine how surprised I was to find out that the FBI had been looking for him for three years. There was a $3,000 reward—and I broke up the biggest counterfeit ring in the country. Boy, was the Chief proud of me!"

*   *   *

It was early in 1937, and "Amos 'n' Andy" had gone over to CBS from NBC. Lou Titterton of NBC was going wild trying to find a replacement for this quarter-hour strip.

Phil Lord had enjoyed great success with "Gangbusters," and had another idea. At the time, Tom Dewey was making big news as the crusading district attorney who fought the Syndicate without fear of the Mafia.

Two or three sample scripts, based on the exploits of a big-city D.A., were written. Putting together a new show starts with meetings—meetings about the idea, the premise, the approach, the story line. During these conferences the series was populated, and all the minor characters were named.

There was a strange development in the character of Mr. District Attorney himself—he never had a name. All through the length of the series he was never called anything but "Chief" by his staff.

This very oddity gave the program its title—"Mr. District Attorney" and no one could remember how the title actually came about or who was responsible for it. The name was used in conversations about the series. Somebody said it once; it was used again; and within a few days everybody referred to the central character as "Mr. D.A." He just happened that way.

"Mr. District Attorney, champion of the people, defender of human rights," later became a popular half-hour weekly series, and starred the very capable actor Jay Jostyn. It was one of many crime series that flooded the air.

Detectives became big business in radio, and nearly every fictional private or public eye had a radio version. There were Ellery Queen, The Shadow, The Green Hornet, The Blue Beetle, The Thin Man, The Fat Man, Mr. and Mrs. North, Mr. Keen—Tracer of Lost Persons, Perry Mason, Philo Vance, Bulldog Drummond, Boston Blackie, Mark Sabre, David Harding, Martin Kane, Mr. Moto, and even Sherlock Holmes.

One of the better-produced half-hour dramas was "Suspense," which used top-flight Hollywood stars, and, while under the aegis of William Spear, paid higher-than-average prices for scripts, which gave him a wide choice of stories by freelance authors, many of whom were really great and gifted writers. Spear's idea was not to create blood and gore for horror's sake—but to build a story around taut suspense . . . a chase, a bungled robbery, a near perfect crime, a series of coincidental mishaps. Some of these "Suspense" scripts found their way into popular classic art forms. One such case was "Sorry, Wrong Number," a thriller originally performed on the radio show as a one-woman monologue by Agnes Moorehead. Although crime seldom, if ever, paid on "Suspense," the William Spear touch was sure—in radio Spear had the same genius that made Hitchcock famous in pictures.

Although the show budgets of the half-hour thriller dramas were limited, the casts small, and the number of suspects in any given situation limited by the number of people in the play, radio was an ideal showcase for them. If you want a haunted house—imagine your own. In the mind's eye could be built the most fantastic and horrible monstrosity.

A few words in the dialogue could conjure the picture of a musty cave, a Park Avenue office, a rainy street, a noisy ginmill. A rolled-up rug was dropped on a studio riser, and a body fell. A mallet crushed a cantaloupe, and a head was bashed in. A foghorn sounded, cleated footsteps on a cement slab, a man whistling were heard—and a detective was strolling along Fishermen's Wharf in San Francisco.

Cook remembers:

*   *   *

The first mystery script I ever sold in my life was to the McCann-Erickson Advertising Agency in 1945. It was for "Dr. Christian," a half-hour drama series for Vaseline products. The show starred Jean Hersholt as Dr. Christian and Rosemary DeCamp as his nurse, Judy Price.

Now, Dr. Christian couldn't be considered a "private

eye" in any sense of the word. He was a good, kindly, conscientious general practitioner of River's End who solved criminal cases only when they came in the line of his day-to-day medical duties. He probably never solved more than a dozen or so murders a year.

The sponsor had a script contest every year. I had become friends with a real-life doctor in Duluth, Minnesota, named Simon Sax who suggested we do a story based on circus characters. He had just treated a couple. He also dug up a beautifully unlikely poison called curare. We were so gone on this poison that we entitled the script "Curare." We were too chicken actually to murder anybody, so we made it an attempted murder.

We had two circus aerialists visit the doctor and complain of dizzy spells and faintness which Dr. Christian immediately diagnosed as polyneuritis. Naturally, he tells them to keep off the trapeze for a while, but they can't afford it. They've slipped from the big time, and now they're playing small towns with one-ring outfits. They need the dough. Dr. Christian insists that they not go on, but they say nuts to him. Just for the heck of it, they leave him two passes for the circus on their way out. Christian asks Judy to go to the circus with him—a good doctor wouldn't be caught dead at a circus without his nurse. As they leave the office, Dr. Christian says mysteriously, "I'd better take my bag with me."

To which Judy replies, "Whatever for? Do you think you'll need it?"

"I have a feeling I just might," Dr. Christian whispers as the organ music puts us in a circus mood.

Wow, huh?

To show that we didn't care what we did with the

sponsor's money, we introduced another character—the circus manager, who quickly explains that he's worried about Benning and Brown—the aerialists. We throw economic caution to the winds and bring in a clown named Jo Jo, their best friend. So now we have a list of suspects that is two people long. Enough.

Benning and Brown do go on, and in the midst of their twists and turns through the air Benning drops Brown.

Guess who's in the house? A doctor! With a nurse and a bag! As the good doctor splints Brown's broken leg, Jo Jo, the clown, acts up to keep the crowd quiet. As he somersaults around the ring, a bottle drops from his pocket. It is labeled "Crude Curare." A clue! Dr. Christian knows what it is immediately—because he's a doctor. He orders the trapeze rig lowered after the crowd is sent home. The dumb River's End constable can't figure out why Dr. Christian insists that Jo Jo, the clown, be arrested . . . and what has crude curare got to do with a circus?

The secret is in the ropes—what has been poured onto them day after day. Though it looks like talcum powder, it's really curare—a deadly poison used by the South American Indians on the tip of the arrows of their blowguns.

Well, they interrogate Jo Jo, and in about forty seconds he breaks down and admits that he's been trying to do away with Benning and Brown for years. He made them big stars—and when he was disabled by a fall it was they who were up there taking the bows.

The final scene in the average radio mystery was a summary, with the lead characters sitting around informally explaining who did what to whom and why. The ending that Dr. Sax and I contrived was of the O. Henry type, and thus not acceptable. There had to be a recapitulation, and somewhere it *had* to be pointed out that crime does not pay.

So, somebody changed the last four lines to incorporate these "must" factors. I have the old script before me—the very script that Vaseline paid a thousand dollars for. Here is the new ending:

JUDY: It was an amazingly ingenious system.

CHRISTIAN: Yes, but that's what defeated him.

JUDY: Only because he dropped the bottle of curare in front of a doctor who recognized it and understood its symptoms. What a break for justice!

CHRISTIAN: Judy, when you've lived as long as I have, you'll find Justice always gets the breaks. (PAUSE) Wrongdoing never pays off in the end.

ORGAN MUSIC . . . RIVER'S END THEME.

After the show I visited Dr. Sax, my collaborator.

"How do you feel?" he asked.

"Well, Doc," I complained, "I've got this pain right here in my neck. . . ."

Networks:
A Multimillion-
Dollar Baby

B Y 1938 four networks were grossing $75,000,000 a year. Looking backward—and not very far at that—the economic rise had been amazing. In a few short years other mass media—newspapers, magazines, and outdoor—had a serious competitor for the national advertising dollar. In 1927 NBC had gross time sales of $3,760,010. The following year it jumped to almost $9,000,000, and moved steadily up year after year.

William Paley's Columbia network had a less lusty 1927—showing a gross of $72,000, but in 1928, $1,447,000 had come in, and ten years later this fledgling was reporting a $27,000,000 annual gross.

The youngest member of the network family—Mutual —was operating by the late thirties, and in 1938 reported well over $2,000,000 in gross revenue. The biggest money-maker was NBC, but this gross was based on the income from two networks—the Red and the Blue. Later, after the government ordered RCA to divest itself of one of them, the Blue Network was purchased by private interests, and became the American Broadcasting Company.

Before the thirties ended, network radio, as a business proposition, was thriving. In only one year, 1931, did the networks fail to pile up grosses to top every other year.

The Mutual Broadcasting System filled a unique niche in the network picture. There had been several unsuccessful efforts to build a fourth chain to compete with NBC's Red and Blue and Columbia. In 1934 an advertiser who wanted to reach Chicago and New York audiences—but didn't want to pay the cost of coast-to-coast network time—approached Newark's WOR and Chicago's WGN. The idea was to air a show over both stations simultaneously, with the program originating in the East. The advertiser paid each station its full, standard card rate. On the basis of that two-station "hookup," Mutual was formed.

WGN and WOR went together on a fifty-fifty basis and sought out advertisers who wanted to use both stations. As a network, MBS was to have no corporate profit. The network officers were paid by the stations for which they worked.

The cooperative grew rapidly as giant 50,000-watters in big markets joined the fold. WLW, "The Nation's Station," in Cincinnati, did a lot for the chain when it became a member. WLW had a few competitors for the title of the most listened-to, most respected station in the country. Its signal at 700 on the dial seemed to reach everywhere.

New England and Midwest stations swelled the growing Mutual ranks, and when the Don Lee Broadcasting System in California joined, it gave the network a coast-to-coast reach. By 1938 Mutual had over a hundred outlets.

The network didn't offer the big glamour stars who were heard often on NBC and CBS, but it did a good solid nuts-and-bolts business with advertisers. MBS could offer advertisers with peculiar marketing problems small "clumps" of stations in a specific national pattern. Mutual could offer regional coverage their competitors couldn't. Mutual also allowed recorded programs that NBC and CBS barred. The major networks were adamant about being "live." They would not allow recorded transition music or sound effects, so Mutual offered advertisers a practicality that was needed in certain areas of broadcasting.

Columbia was the network to watch in the mid-thirties. Paley was piling up great profits on his original premise—that money could be made in chain radio. By 1938 many blue-chip advertisers were in his camp. "The Lux Radio Theatre" had switched over to CBS from NBC. "The Ford Sunday Evening Hour" had become a big favorite, and Burns and Allen were on Columbia sponsored by Chesterfield. Palmolive Shave Cream presented "Gangbusters" on CBS. Texaco and Old Gold cigarettes were on the rolls. Paley's star lineup included Al Jolson, Eddie Cantor, Kate Smith, Robert Benchley, Max Reinhardt, and Lum 'n' Abner.

Network radio was the new darling of mass media, and advertisers were making it a very rich and splendid thing.

Naturally, competition for the audience was becoming a great and serious war. The John Royal versus Bill Paley program battle of the early thirties was a game of tag compared to the knock-down, drag-out fight that happened a decade later.

To start at the end, William Paley won the final round of the tug of war between NBC and CBS in 1948. He introduced a new phrase to broadcasting: "Capital gains." Big-time entertainers were feeling the effects of the government's big tax bite on their astronomical salaries, and this was the crowbar Paley used to pry the big ones loose from the NBC roster. To oversimplify it, "Amos 'n' Andy" was a corporation in which Amos per se and Andy per se were merely parts. Any profits made by the Amos 'n' Andy corporation were capital gains, and subject to only a 25 percent tax, while Gosden and Correll as individuals would give the government up to 90 percent of what they earned as salary. Paley bought the Amos 'n' Andy corporation for $2,000,000 and brought the entire property over to Columbia lock, stock, and Kingfish.

Paley bought the Jack Benny corporation.

He bought the Edgar Bergen corporation.

He bought NBC's Sunday night.

In retrospect it seems that Paley's primary concentration was on programming, while NBC—a sliver of the giant known as RCA—had other interests. Columbia's only concern was being a network, which undoubtedly gave Paley a leg up.

In the late thirties Columbia had a network of 114 stations. NBC was a bigger chain because it was actually two. However, the Blue Network of NBC could not completely blanket the nation when the Red Network was sold out because it shared its stations in many cases. CBS and NBC Red were the real competitors for the advertising dollar and the big star.

Networks: A Multimillion-Dollar Baby

CBS was not too proud to accept second-hand hits from NBC, such as Major Bowes and Fred Allen. Often shows picked up remarkably after they had had a long run on the opposition network and for all intents were dead issues when they switched to Columbia.

CBS built new shows from the ground up, too. They brought Texaco and P. Lorillard into the fold before the exact show formats were set, and surprised a delighted nation with a variety of formats that included Robert Benchley, Adolphe Menjou, Una Merkel, Charlie Ruggles, Jane Froman, and Kenny Baker.

In 1938 over half of Columbia's time was sustaining, and Paley took great pride in the program fare that filled the noncommercial hours. There was the "Mercury Theatre," the spawning ground of Orson Welles, Joseph Cotton, and so many greats of the theater and motion pictures. "The American School of the Air," "College Bull Session," "Backgrounds of Literature," and "Capitol Cloakroom" were highly respected by their small audiences. But at the sustaining level Columbia offered entertainment, too. Two decades before Mitch Miller, CBS listeners were singing along with the Landt Trio and enjoying a quarter-hour afternoon show featuring a pleasant-voiced young man from Chicago by the name of Perry Como. Yes, Como was once sustaining.

By the middle thirties President Paley was the highest-paid executive in radio, receiving $169,097 in salary and bonuses. CBS profits were high, too.

Paley was concerned for the growth of the industry. He was more than merely an efficient operator. In April of 1938, the Federal Communications Commission investigated network operations, and the youthful dynamo aired radio's case to the public over the network in his annual report as Columbia's president.

He urged that regulations be kept to the minimum in order to keep radio reception free from government interference.

He hired Paul White, an experienced United Press news executive, to head his news operation, and inaugurated the world news roundup, with correspondents reporting from all over the world.

Audience gains and profit gains were synonomous in Paley's mind. Columbia had sold $7,500,000 worth of time in 1930—while NBC's sales were nearly three times that amount. Paley's salesmen were having a tough time explaining away why NBC programs were at the top of the rating lists.

He called in an associate by the name of Paul Kesten who conceived the first study of network popularity.

The accounting firm of Price, Waterhouse and Company was employed to send 200,000 cards to radio owners in 67 cities asking, "What radio station do you listen to most?"

The answers showed that CBS affiliates were listened to more frequently than other stations. That bit of information helped boost the 1931 sales of CBS to nearly $12,000,-000—despite the depression.

All through the years of rough economy, networks were prospering, but none understood the economic phenomenon of this great new advertising force so clearly as William Samuel Paley and his Columbia Broadcasting System.

The Backyard Fiction

A n d now—Portia Faces Life!

ORGAN MUSIC.

Portia's heart tightened sickeningly as she saw the fear grow in Mark Randall's face. Could she tell him his chances of proving his innocence were desperately slim? That everything depended on Bill Baker being able to bring Kathie to the courtroom before Joan took the stand? What can she say—as once more Mark demands . . .

"If something's gone wrong . . . For God's sake, Portia, don't just sit there like that!"

Whether the inventor of the soap opera deserves credit or blame is a moot point—particularly when it is quite impossible to nail down the exact emergence of this form of backyard fiction. The fifteen-minute, five-day-a-week drama program found tremendous popularity when the comedy team of Charles Correll and Freeman Gosden turned "Amos 'n' Andy" into a national institution. Their comedy was serialized, and its suspense was strong enough to cause President Calvin Coolidge to issue an order that he was not to be disturbed during the time "Amos 'n' Andy" was on the air.

On the heels of the success of the proprietors of the Fresh Air Taxicab Company came such early serial dramas as "The Rise of the Goldbergs," "Myrt and Marge," and "Easy Aces." These programs weren't "soap operas" in the truest sense, for they were based on the platform of comedy. In fact, some of the finest comedy of all time came from the pens of Goodman Ace and Gertrude Berg.

Avid listeners of the day will never forget Jane Ace's malaprops such as, "Well, you could have knocked me over with a fender," or, "When I get the urge, I'm completely uninhabited!"

There was Gertrude Berg's welcome "Yoo hoo! Is anybody?" that started each program in the warm and funny Goldbergs series.

But Amos 'n' Andy were the kings. Their expressions were imitated by nearly every man, woman, and child who ever got near a radio:

"I'se regusted!"

"Ow wah! Ow wah!"

"I want you to know that my wife is very unhappy!"

"Buzz me, Miss Blue!"

"Check and double check."

The mythical Harlem neighborhood teemed with wildly wonderful characters—Madame Queen, Lightnin', Brother Crawford, George Stevens—the Kingfish of the Mystic Knights of the Sea, and Andy's secretary, Miss Blue.

Gosden and Correll first got together in 1919 and started a burnt-cork vaudeville team called "Sam 'n' Henry." In 1926 "Sam 'n' Henry" made its debut as a local program over WMAQ. Two years later they changed the name of the act to "Amos 'n' Andy," and went network.

In 1931 *Variety*—the show-business newspaper—said, in a formal review of the "Amos 'n' Andy" show:

Amos 'n' Andy . . . have the greatest number of authorized —and unauthorized—articles named after them, get the largest salary of any team broadcasting, share with Rudy Vallee the distinction of being the only radio attraction to be starred in a talking picture.

They are being imitated nightly; female counterparts have sprung up, mixed teams are numerous, whole family groups are gabbing, all inspired, directly or indirectly, by Amos 'n' Andy.

Episodic conversation, 15 minutes a night, has been a recognized entertainment form of radio. Some programs start out well but quickly stale. Few have sufficient wind to stand the long night-after-night grind. Freshness is lost, real humor is replaced by straining effort. That is why the Amos 'n' Andy scripts, self-written and self-staged, are the classics of the industry.

At present their stride is slow and their wit dulled as if in exhaustion from the previous pace. They have lately been concerning themselves with an asinine routine about Andy, the shiftless member, writing his life story for a newspaper syndicate. Here the boys have gotten out of contact with common sense and the everyday touch. The sooner they get back to the orbit of average experience, the securer will be their position.

And while suggesting improvements to the auspices it is apropos to allude to a pronounced tendency of Pepsodent to oversell. Their copy is pleonasmic and gushy. More than a few will realize that they take advantage of the audience held to attention by the pending arrival of their favorites to jam through an unusually large big dose of commercialism.

Pepsodent theme song is now played by a studio orchestra where formerly it was a phonograph record. It is no exaggeration to tag "The Perfect Song" the best known and most quickly identified theme number on the air.

Let it be for the record that "Amos 'n' Andy" was the most successful, most talked-about and quoted fifteen-minute strip on the air—ever. Only after many years did the famous team "retire" to a half-hour, once-a-week nighttime format on NBC adjacent to "Fibber McGee and Molly" on NBC's powerful Tuesday-night lineup of the middle and late forties.

Amos 'n' Andy's first—and only—motion picture, *Check and Double Check,* was a monument to mediocrity—a Hollywood device of the 1930's of using famous names for marquee value only, and hanging weak stories on them.

CBS lured Amos 'n' Andy away from NBC in 1948 with an unprecedented capital-gains deal. Because of high taxes, the capital-gains arrangement was very beneficial to artists who formed their own companies. The network actually bought the stars' company, and the star went along with the deal as an "employee." Later, NBC was to have its applecart of talent upset again with further star acquisitions by Columbia.

In their latter radio days, and on their entrance into television, the team met some stiff publicity opposition from such groups as the National Association for the Advancement of Colored People who felt that Amos 'n' Andy's interpretation of Negro life did not depict the Negro in his best light, that the characters and the situations—although comedic in every sense—were unfair to the race. The scheming Kingfish, ignorant Lightnin', slow-witted Andy, and flouncy Madame Queen were not considered in any way typical of Negroes in America. And, to be sure, they were not—any more than Red Skelton's Freddy the Freeloader or Willie Lump-Lump are typical of American whites.

Amos 'n' Andy, along with the continuity acceptance boards of the networks for whom they broadcast, bowed to the "change in thinking," and their nighttime half-hour found supporting roles in the series filled by Negroes. The era of the white man donning blackface, so standard in the vaudeville days, was gone forever.

When "Amos 'n' Andy" was transferred to television, Freeman Gosden and Charles Correll did not appear at all. They, too, were replaced by Negroes.

The burnt-cork offerings of Jolson and Cantor who had risen to fame in blackface had disappeared, too—as did the wonderful old minstrel shows.

Amos 'n' Andy had the fifteen-minute serial field all to themselves for a very short time. Suddenly, in the early thirties, there was an epidemic of quarter-hour programs, but with few exceptions they were far from being comedy programs.

The soap opera itself—or washboard weeper—was probably born in Chicago, which at one time was considered the heart and soul of network radio.

From the Merchandise Mart and the Wrigley Building came a horde of new titles and tribulations—"Ma Perkins," "Bachelor's Children," "Portia Faces Life," "The Guiding Light," "Against the Storm," "The Right to Happiness" —close to a hundred of them.

It Sounds Impossible

Chicago was the breeding ground for this type of radio probably because this was the city that contained the talent that really developed the first radio entertainment forms. "Amos 'n' Andy" started there. So did "Fibber Mc-Gee and Molly" and "The First Nighter." The early-evening children's serial originated in Chicago with "Little Orphan Annie," "Tom Mix," and "Captain Midnight."

It is doubtful that you will ever hear another "soap opera" on radio—but their part in the history of the medium is undeniable. By 1938 there were seventy-eight such programs on the air—all sponsored and each with a "following."

What they *were* is really more interesting than what they were *about*.

The stories were, for the most part, depressing. They were often badly written; they dragged, and one tale followed another on the air in weary and continuous sequence. NBC scheduled as many as twelve of them back-to-back in the late afternoon. Columbia offered the same static pattern. ABC got into the act, too, although not on quite so large a scale.

The serial stories dominated the program schedules all day for most of the week.

Some of the dramas were really dreadful, and some were even salacious.

The daytime serial became, by the late thirties, the most-criticized form of radio entertainment—and one of the most loyally followed. Audiences numbered in the millions.

The soap opera helped the housewife time her day. She would sit down to her second cup of coffee with "Betty and Bob," wash the breakfast dishes to "Judy and Jane,"

The Backyard Fiction

pick up the living room through "Our Gal Sunday," and start lunch with "Helen Trent." She'd start the kids back to school with "Vic and Sade," scrub the kitchen floor to "Road of Life," make out the grocery list to "Right to Happiness," and start peeling potatoes for supper with "Just Plain Bill."

Young marrieds today don't know of that erstwhile all-American homemaker's schedule. Television, we are sure, will never quite fill that void.

Frank and Ann Hummert were probably the true parents of the daytime serial. They created more of them than any other production team. The Hummerts had as many as a dozen such programs on the air at one time, accounting for three full hours of network programming daily.

Mild-looking, bespectacled Frank Hummert, a former St. Louis newspaperman, switched to radio in 1927 as copy chief for the Blackett and Sample advertising agency in Chicago. Anne Ashenhurst was hired as his assistant three years later. The fact that Anne was the first woman he could ever tolerate around an office undoubtedly had something to do with their later marriage. Between them they worked out their first two daytime serials—"Betty and Bob" and "Just Plain Bill." By 1935 they were being paid about $150,000 a year. During that time they had as many as sixty-seven shows a week on the networks.

Hummert productions filled some $9,000,000 worth of airtime a year during radio's golden age. The name Hummert was added to the company banner—and Blackett-Sample-Hummert, Inc., was the nation's Number One buyer of radio time and the Number One supplier of program material.

Each program had its own writer—not author—*writer.*

It Sounds Impossible

The Hummerts personally supervised the scripts on all their shows. Frank and Anne gave the world "John's Other Wife," "Second Husband," "The Romance of Helen Trent," "Lorenzo Jones," "Mary Noble—Backstage Wife," "Our Gal Sunday," "Young Widder Brown," "Stella Dallas," "David Harum" and—of course!—many others.

Frank and Anne, working from their Greenwich, Connecticut, home, would figure out the story outlines for their dozen or so dramatic properties, working from four to six weeks in advance. These outlines were dictated to a battery of stenographers.

A typical story line might read like this (the plot is the work of the authors of this book, not of Frank and Anne):

Suspecting that Reggie Downs murdered Ann Finster's cousin Bert after a row at the Grandhaven Country Club, Mayme Dixon calls on kindly attorney Ben Smythe to do some investigating on the side. The lawyer hires Fred Strong, a private eye, to help him with the inquiries. Mayme decides to work her own way, and tries to talk to Tess Baker, Reggie's sister-in-law, at her fashionable penthouse apartment, but, upon arrival, Mayme is denied entrance by Tess's butler. Lawyer Smythe finds a clue, a cigarette lighter stuffed behind a chair in the murder room. It bears the initials *M.D.* Can this mean Mayme Dixon? Is that why she is so anxious to have someone else pointed out as the possible killer? Will this cause Lawyer Smythe to drop the investigation? Will Fred Strong go ahead on his own?

A ghost-writer then took over and finished off the script with dialogue, sound effects, organ stingers—the works. By hiring writers—not creators—the Hummerts saved a great

deal of money. In 1939 they were paying a minimum of
$25 per dramatic script, while most serial writers were
averaging about $200 to $400 a week, and specialists like
Gertrude Berg earned about $2,000 a week. Hummert
writers seemed happy, though, for they could do other
writing assignments on the side. Their factory produced
some good radio writers, too, and afforded a talented
writer a chance to run up a few credits.

Advertising agencies and their creative staffs had a considerable voice in the development of the soap opera.
Their bounden duty was to supply a radio vehicle that
would sell laundry soap or toothpaste or cleanser or sham-
poo. Some became experts in the field.

Such a man was Max Wylie, one of the most talented
and influential ad-agency men in the radio and television
business, presently with the firm of Lennen & Newell, Inc.
More than merely a good producer, director, and writer,
Max was, and is, a student of mass media, and is one of the
rarities who can look a production in its economic and
artistic face and know whether it has the required mass appeal to (*a*) succeed as a program and (*b*) sell the product
his agency represents.

Max was closely associated with the daytime serial during its heyday.

He often pointed out that the psychology of the soap
opera was not too complicated—women have to be top-dog
all the time, even when they are the underdog. They have
to "suffer." Most of the soap operas made the women feel
superior to mere man, or ill used by man. The women-
heroines went on valiantly in the face of the most overwhelming obstacles.

It Sounds Impossible

There was even one daytimer called "Valiant Lady" for rather obvious reasons.

Often the heroines had man-sized jobs. Portia, for example, was a very successful lawyer, and old Ma Perkins was the dynamic operator of a lumberyard.

Wylie believes that these shows met a tremendous need that no other medium in American life offered.

"There was a common complaint," Max recalls. "It seemed that everybody wanted to know why we didn't have shows about happy homes and happy people.

"We had a few—a very few—and they were comedy shows. Most of the shows were about unhappy homes and unhappy people. The main reason, of course, why radio had so many stories about trouble-ridden families is that the picture of the well-adjusted family presented no problem and hence no story."

Soap-opera producers of the day presumed that most people were more preoccupied with the unhappy aspects of their lives and past recollections, and thought more about the uncertainty of their futures than they did about the occasional happy moments of their existence.

The axiom was obvious—misery loved company.

Max Wylie projected another thought when discussing the radio soap opera in retrospect and the development of the television soap opera of today.

He believes that women of the daytime audiences have physical and psychic problems that they themselves cannot understand, and cannot solve. Being physical, they feel the thrust of these problems. Being poor, they cannot buy remedies in the form of doctors, new clothes, or fancy coiffures; being unanalytical, they cannot figure out what is really the matter with them; and being inarticulate, they cannot explain their problem even if they know what it is. The radio soap opera—as does the TV serial today—presented more difficult and complicated problems than those vexing the listener. Or it kept them away from their problems.

So with "Helen Trent" and "Our Gal Sunday" the listeners had two constant and frequently simultaneous choices—participation or escape. Both worked.

This is what soap operas were. What they were *about* is something else again.

They were about adultery, unwed motherhood, murder, acid-throwing, broken legs, forgery, greed, auto accidents, fires, in-law trouble, divorce, status frustrations, jealousy, robbery, babies, bitchy women, weak-willed men, drunkenness, business failure, suicide, and love. Oh, there was a lot of love.

Many soap operas opened with a long synopsis of current events. Frank and Anne Hummert never knew that an announcer on one of their NBC daytimers carried a pencil to the microphone with him each day. He had it sharpened to a needlelike point. When he would start the synopsis, at the beginning of each show, he would press the point into his thumb. The longer the synopsis, the sharper the pressure on his thumb would become. The reason he did so was that he was deathly afraid of collapsing with laughter when he was halfway through the complicated updating. The pain in his thumb kept his mind off the ridiculousness of the situation.

The program openings never changed on some shows. Day after day, week after week, year after year, millions of commiserators would hear:

" 'Our . . . Gal . . . Sunday'! The story of an orphan girl named Sunday, from the little mining town of Silver

Creek, Colorado, who in young womanhood married England's richest, most handsome lord, Lord Henry Brinthrope. The story asks: *CAN* this girl from a mining town in the West find happiness as the wife of a wealthy and *titled* Englishman?"

The daily answer led you to believe that she never would, no matter how hard she tried.

While this show was still numbered among the most popular on the daytime air, the comedy team of Bob and Ray came out with a parody on two Hummert serials—"Mary Noble, Backstage Wife" and "Our Gal Sunday." Their introduction went something like this:

"Next, for all her friends waiting for her on their radios, Mary Backstage, Noble Wife, the true-life interesting story of a girl from a deserted mining town out west who came to the city to seek happiness and security as the wife of handsome Harry Backstage—Broadway star—and what it means to be the wife of the idol of a million other women."

To a select audience the day-to-day Bob and Ray sketches were hilarious. The speech patterns of the characters, the very plots themselves were frighteningly close to the story outlines put forth by the original authors. Many soap-opera fans resented Bob and Ray's wry approach to something they held sacred. As a result, Bob and Ray never won a Hooper rating as high as those of the actual soap operas during the heyday of the daytime serial.

Some of the great names in motion pictures and the stage came out of the Chicago soap-opera cradle. John Hodiak was a veteran of the washboard weepers, as were Macdonald Carey, Richard Widmark, Martha Scott, Frank Lovejoy, Jim Backus, and Tyrone Power. The Chicago radio-actors club also included Don Ameche, Garry Moore, Red Skelton, Durward Kirby, Mercedes McCambridge, and Art Carney.

If there was a "typical" big-time radio actress of the era it would be Fran Carlon. To listeners she was Bunny Mitchell in "Mary Marlin." She was Lorelei Kilborne, ace assistant and girl Friday to Steve Wilson of the Big Town Illustrated Press. She played on "Stella Dallas," "Portia Faces Life," "Backstage Wife," "Manhattan Mother," "David Harum"—you name it. She's on many television commercials these days, and on the Broadway stage.

Fran agrees that an era in radio has passed that will never return. "But it's a shame," she said. "Radio drama made people use their imaginations. Television will never be able to recreate what a housewife could see in her mind's eye when the announcer, during the prologue, would say softly:

" 'Bunny Mitchell sweeps down the exquisite staircase at her hilltop mansion in Alexandria. She wears the gown that Fraser loves best. . . .' Every housewife listening built her own scene. Television couldn't afford such a lovely staircase."

Fran, who did "Portia Faces Life" on TV when that show entered the new medium, maintains that, instead of building dream castles in a woman's mind, you had a real architectural situation with a real set and real budget problems.

"Consequently," she said, "the show lost a great deal. This was it. This was the living room of the house. There was no imagining, and the wonderful make-believe was gone. The drama emerged as a daytime television show with a budget problem."

It Sounds Impossible

There were five around the table in the back room of Louis and Armand, a favorite CBS hangout—five stalwarts who had smiled through vales and vales of tears on "Right to Happiness," "Ma Perkins," "David Harum," "Helen Trent," "Big Sister," and "Wendy Warren." We had been across the street in a studio they all knew well—famous Number Seven at CBS where they had just taped a rather cheerful discussion about soap operas. This was something of a wake—with real liquor.

They were fairly typical of the featured radio actors of the soap-opera era. Their capabilities, backgrounds, and talents often went undetected in the roles they were asked to portray—and their characterizations in radio were ill remembered because much of the writing they read was written to be forgotten; but, at one time, these people commanded more attention and bigger audiences than many Broadway stars ever enjoyed.

Clockwise around the table were:

Paul McGrath—tall, handsome, graying temples and a well-trimmed gray moustache. His smile was easy and his manner most affable. A truly fine and distinguished actor of stage, motion pictures, and television, he played the romantic lead in a number of soap operas and is probably best remembered for his long "run" in Rinso's "Big Sister" and as the host in "Inner Sanctum."

Next to Paul was Claudia Morgan, daughter of film star Ralph Morgan and niece of the late beloved Frank Morgan. It was Claudia who brought the sexy signature to the half-hour detective drama when, as Nora Charles on "Adventures of the Thin Man," she ended each episode with the phrase that caused millions of virile young American men to whistle—her famous, "Good night, Nicky darling!" Claudia was heard most regularly on "Right to

176

Happiness." She, like the men of the Morgan dynasty, got her training in the theater. A truly beautiful woman, with the strong, outgoing personality that was the mark of a Morgan.

There was Art Hanna—producer, director, actor, a graduate of "Ma Perkins," "Our Gal Sunday," and a dozen others.

Kay Campbell, who had played Evie Fitz in "Ma Perkins," was there. It was obvious that Kay never suffered the way Evie did—and that she had far fewer emotional problems.

And at the end of the table was Bill Adams, who looked as fine and good and kindly as all the roles he had ever portrayed on the radio. Although Bill was in a raft of soaps, he is probably best remembered as the Uncle Bill of "Let's Pretend," a weekly visit he made to listeners for twenty-five years. Bill's first radio role was in a Shakespearian play broadcast back in 1924. Shortly afterward he played in the first radio broadcast of *Uncle Tom's Cabin,* which originated in Gimbel's department store. Bill was John Barrymore's personal director when the Great Profile played Shakespeare in England.

These were not bland people; they were excellent actors and actresses, knowledgeable and highly intelligent individuals who worked radio for fun, for an often-expressed hope that radio drama would raise its standards, and, most of all, for money. Radio paid well for the amount of work involved. The hours were great. Because actors could work directly from a script, line learning was unnecessary. There were generally only two or three read-through rehearsals before airtime. But in some respects it was still a job of work.

"We get back to this illusion thing," Art Hanna said,

"the mental picture. There were no aids—no props. Just the fantastic concentration on voice and nuance. We had to illustrate with sound—only sound."

"And the parts we were asked to play!" said Bill Adams. "Why, I remember that back in the early days of 'The March of Time' one evening I'd play Hindenburg and the next week I'd be some country doctor who took out his own appendix. They had me do Franklin Roosevelt a lot. I'll never forget the day he was elected. . . . I was asked to do his voice on the radio. I did it several times after that."

We were all a little surprised. Bill's voice is low and modulated—Roosevelt's was several tones higher.

"He was a performer with his voice," Bill said. "And he wasn't too difficult to imitate."

"Do Roosevelt for us!" Claudia Morgan insisted.

"No, sir," Bill answered.

"Why not?" I asked.

"I don't do Roosevelt for free. I'm a Republican!"

Soap-opera scripting was often a matter of economy. The production costs on a given episode were less when fewer actors were needed. This bit of economic expediency frequently upset Bill Adams who was the kindly doctor on "Ma Perkins."

"I was the best doggone doctor in the entire world," Bill said. "I don't care whether Ma had a broken back or Evie had the black plague. By golly, when I came into the scene everybody was cured almost instantly. But this was very bad for me. It meant I worked only one or two episodes."

The talk drifted to the slips, the goofs, and the wonderfully wild things that could happen only in live radio—

when the difference in time across the nation meant a repeat performance for the West Coast.

Paul McGrath remembered several times when the story line or the budget or both had only two actors in an episode. Once, during "Big Sister," he was doing a heavily emotional love scene with the heroine. In the fixing and cutting of scenes, and in the mimeographing of the final script, you might find lines in the story that used up only a third of a page. Generally, the thoughtful typist writes the word "more" at the bottom of the page. This time she didn't.

Paul's heroine came to the end of that particular page and, as the organ played the transitional interlude, she left the studio with five minutes of love yet to be made. So Paul The Trouper whispered sweet nothings to a microphone until closing-theme time.

"I guess everybody used to wonder," we said, "if anybody ever showed up at a live dramatic program crocked to the eyeballs."

"Not often," Art Hanna said. "Only often enough to make it memorable."

"Whenever that happened, it was generally between the first show and the West Coast repeat," Claudia said. "Some poor guy would have a few hours to kill, and a pal would ask him to have a drink . . . and sometimes that led to two or three or four. Of course, the second show was not quite the same as the original."

The wonderful real people who populated the worlds of the long-suffering soap-opera characters: real, important people, in hardly real, unimportant dramas that were ground out of control rooms in New York and Chicago by the score.

It Sounds Impossible

Of all the daytime dramas, one stood out like a ruby in a bag of marbles. It was "Vic and Sade"; but it was not a true serial in the cliff-hanger sense. It had to do with a middle-class Midwestern family with middle-class Midwestern problems that were magnified ever so slightly and very artfully by one of the greatest comedy writers of all time—Paul Rymer. Rymer had a deep understanding of the average man. Each day's story was a little gem unto itself. It might have been Vic, the husband and father, thumbing through a catalogue for his lodge—wishing he could buy every cap, uniform, and official scepter in the book. It might have been Sade on the phone discussing a washrag sale at Yamelton's department store. Or it might have the son, Rush, telling about his encounter with his pal, Blue Tooth Johnson. Or Uncle Fletcher explaining why he was a daily guest aboard Mr. Gumpox's garbage wagon, and why he found philosophical solace in riding the garbage route with Mr. Gumpox. Sometimes it was a long-distance phone call from Ishigan Fishigan of Sishigan, Michigan, or a telegram from Robert and Slobbert Hink, identical twins whom Vic and Sade had met on vacation.

The greatest of the characterizations was Uncle Fletcher. Everybody has an Uncle Fletcher. He didn't hear too well —either that or he could successfully ignore what was being said. He reminisced constantly, to Sade's despair—generally ending up with something like: "I wonder sometimes whatever happened to Ardmore Ruler after he sold his buttermilk and cottage-cheese store in Blue Haven, Pennsylvania. I know that his brother Harty moved to Walla Walla, Washington, after Ardmore left Blue Haven, married a woman fourteen years of age—later died."

Uncle Fletcher's answer for everything was "Fine!" If

The Backyard Ficton

Vic said, "I saw you on Mr. Gumpox's garbage wagon today, Uncle Fletcher," Uncle Fletcher would respond with
"Fine!" Or if Sade said, "Would you mind not inviting
your friends to sleep on our davenport, Uncle Fletcher?"

"Fine, Sadie, fine."

Ah, Vic, ah, Sade—how sad that you've gone!

CHAPTER 17

Radio's Finest Hour

B O B T R O U T sat on a straight-backed chair at the end of a long bank of teletype machines on the seventeenth floor of the CBS building on Madison Avenue. He wasn't bored, although he'd been sitting in that same chair holding a microphone for nearly four days, waiting for a single flash from the machines—or one word from a contemporary in the CBS newsroom.

The date: August 14, 1945.

Trout's most memorable news report began building up on the preceding Friday—the 10th. It was the 1,343rd day of the Allied war with Japan. Newscaster Allen Jackson cut in on the Arthur Godfrey morning show to read a United Press bulletin:

"Tokyo Radio says Japan will accept the Potsdam ultimatum if the prerogatives of the Emperor are not compromised."

For the next four days the news was charged with tension. It looked like the end of the war—but nothing was official. Until it was, fighting continued.

Trout was chosen by CBS to deliver the official V-J word to its radio audience the moment the White House issued the announcement, and when he was not on the air with a news analysis or special report he sat in the wooden chair. He was not allowed to go out to eat. Plate dinners and sandwiches were sent in. Whenever he decided he had to go to the washroom, news writers and secretaries held doors open for him—and kept them open until he returned. If the flash should come, CBS didn't want Trout to be running into doorknob trouble. Bob recalls that there were four doors he had to pass through between the CBS newsroom and its men's-room facilities.

This was the culmination of a siege for Trout. He probably had been on the network air more than any other newsman during World War II—was at the microphone longer, had been in on more world-shaking events, and, as a consequence, had eaten more sandwiches out of paper bags and drunk more coffee out of paper cups than any living American of the day.

At 9:34 on the night of Sunday, August 12th, Bob was scanning the teletypes, checking the tenor of the stories coming out of the wire services, when the United Press machine broke loose with a barrage of bells. They were the low-toned "flash bells" as opposed to the higher-sounding "bulletin bells" which had rung so repeatedly during the last few years.

> *FLASH:* VICTORY IN JAPAN.
> TRUMAN AGREES TO TREATY.

Once before, while the nation was on tenterhooks awaiting the word that the D-Day invasion had begun, the Associated Press had sent a false flash. A teletype operator by the name of Joan Ellis somehow—it's never been explained *exactly* how—put the phony story out on the Saturday before D-Day. It was not only embarrassing but actually quite dangerous in time of war.

Trout's first reaction, therefore, was not elation but caution.

"I went on the air right from the teletype," Bob said. "I cautioned the audience that so far only the United Press had the flash. The other machines now were silent. There was just a hum in the newsroom—no clatter of keys. Then the UP machine started up again. I said that another flash was coming in on United Press. I held the microphone down near the teletype so that they could hear the ringing of the flash bells, and I read the words as they appeared on the paper."

FLASH! EDITORS: HOLD UP THAT FLASH!

"That was 9:36. There was deathly silence in the newsroom. Associated Press still and blank. Reuters—quiet. Only the hum again. The last time there had been a hold on a flash was on the Joan Ellis goof. Now the Washington Bureau of UP came on and said their earlier report was erroneous and that they had not sent a flash and were investigating its origin.

"International News Service then opened up to say that the UP flash was in error.

"We went off the air from the newsroom at 9:42—awaiting further word. It was a very quick broadcast—a few short minutes out of a broadcast day; but what happened next really made me realize the power of our medium.

"I remember going to the window on the seventeenth floor and sticking my head out. The tugs were whistling, and people were blowing automobile horns. People were shouting; the town suddenly came alive—and I remember thinking: This is terrible, horrible! I cautioned the people. This is not the end of the war, I told them. This is only something on UP. And I said to myself, My God, what have we done here?"

Bob Trout is known in the business as a very cool newsman. He never gets in the way of the news he reports. The very last thing you expect from Trout is emotion under tension. This was one of the reasons he was selected by Paul White, then director of CBS News, to handle the most important announcements on the air. When Bob "tenses up" he automatically develops a sort of keenness about his job. He admitted that once he finally realized the importance of what he was saying, "I suddenly got that feeling, and I guess there was a catch in my voice. It even startled me a bit.

"It started building up right after that United Press thing. I did all my usual news-analysis broadcasts, but between times I was still glued to that chair."

Paul White—during the early war years—had an electronic device built for his desk that was probably the forerunner of all electric brains. He called it his "piano." With the touch of a button he could talk to Washington, Paris, London, anywhere CBS could string a line or set up a transmitter. Sitting behind his news director's desk, he could literally monitor the world.

At 6:53 on the morning of Tuesday, August 14th, White got on his "piano" for a talk with Dick Hottelet in London. Hottelet seemed to think that the surrender terms had finally been accepted and that the people of London had worn themselves down after three days of celebrating.

"I don't know why," Bob Trout said, "but I kind of

had the feeling when I heard Hottelet and White talking that something was about to happen. It did—but not until seven o'clock that night."

White suddenly ordered a phone installed next to the bank of teletypes. It was a special line to the White House. Bill Henry was covering that area for CBS. All radio newsrooms had been told to stand by "for an official statement from the President to be released at 7:00 P.M. Eastern War Time."

A message on the "piano" from London: "The Prime Minister will broadcast from Number 10 Downing Street at seven o'clock your time."

"Looking back, it might seem a little corny now," Bob said, "but here's what I said at seven:

" 'This is the supreme hour, seven o'clock Eastern War Time. The correspondents at the White House have entered President Truman's office, and the Prime Minister of Great Britain is about to begin his broadcast, so without further ado, we take you to London.'

"I heard Big Ben striking eight times. I looked at Paul who was on the phone in the newsroom and he hollered to me, 'Full acceptance! Go ahead!'

"I started out again:

" 'The Japanese have accepted our terms fully: that is the word we just received from the White House in Washington. And I didn't expect to hear a celebration here in our newsroom in New York, but you can hear one going on behind me.'

"We switched," Bob said, "but I'm not sure what happened. I'm not sure whether we heard the first words of Prime Minister Atlee or not. I couldn't hear anything on the speaker in my studio and I was a little confused—but thrilled.

"The newsroom and the studio areas were going wild. The noise had started down in the streets.

"Then," Trout said, "a strange thought struck me. In one way—I thought—this is ludicrous. Here's the war coming to a great end—after fighting all over the world, and the whole center of the thing, as far as the CBS network is concerned, is me standing here with a little microphone in a room on Madison Avenue.

"And this room always has been the center—on the seventeenth floor. It doesn't look like anything—you say, 'This is part of the whole broadcasting effort—so what?' It's a room. Shouldn't I be out in the mud or on a ship or something?"

When war broke out in Europe in 1939, the newest— and soon to become the biggest—stars in show business were the network newscasters. By the time Pearl Harbor happened, radio had catapulted itself to new heights in the esteem of the American citizenry. From the standpoint of thoughtful service and showmanship, it was radio's finest hour. A great country was in need of the best and fastest informational news service ever devised—and radio came through.

But early broadcasters were a little slow in realizing the importance of news. The beginnings were all local.

Early in 1923, Bill Slocum, of the New York *Herald Tribune*, broadcast a fifteen-minute news summary over WJZ, and in October, H. V. Kaltenborn, then editor of the Brooklyn *Eagle*, began a weekly series of "current events" over WEAF. His first program commented sharply on prohibition, Lloyd George, and the problems in the Rhineland. H.V., "dean of the commentators," joined CBS in 1929. During the Munich crisis and the war years with

It Sounds Impossible

NBC, H.V.'s nasal tones and sometimes odd pronunciation became known to millions of listeners.

But the majority of the several hundred radio stations on the air in the 1920's simply ignored regular news summaries, and concentrated on music, entertainment, special events and sports which really provided the impetus for today's tremendous news operations.

It wasn't until about the time of Roosevelt's election that network news began to take shape and develop. Slate was on the original staff of the Columbia News Service, the first radio news organization:

*   *   *

Sam Slate remembers . . .

It was September of 1933, and I was in New York on vacation. I'd gone to see my first network radio program, featuring Will Rogers. I don't remember much about the show except that Rogers timed his portion by hanging an alarm clock on a stand mike.

After the broadcast, in a crowded descending elevator at 485 Madison Avenue, I heard someone say, "Hello there, Paul White."

"Are you Paul White, formerly with the UP?" I asked. He was a six-footer, with light brown hair combed straight back in a depression-day pompadour, and a wide, smiling mouth.

White nodded, and I introduced myself as "SS of AJ" —my initials and the code letter of the Atlanta office of the United Press. That was how we identified ourselves on the UP teletype. White was "PW of NX" (New York). These symbols were always used in sending messages on the wires. I'd exchanged scores of such messages with White, and talked with him often on the telephone, but we'd never met before.

The next morning I went to see Paul in his office, and heard his plans for the formation of a radio news agency—the Columbia News Service. It sounded exciting, so I asked for a job, and got it.

Until then radio news was, at best, a sometime thing.

For instance, there was the kidnapping of the Lindbergh baby in 1932. The first news of that sensational crime reached New York stations by phone from the Newark papers, which performed this courtesy service for a credit line at the end of the bulletin. Most of the stations used the story, and CBS sent technicians and broadcasters to police headquarters in Trenton and even to the Lindbergh estate. NBC didn't carry the story. It was considered "too sensational."

Newspapers had been among the first to encourage and nurse the infant radio industry. After the stock-market crash of 1929, when radio began to take advertising revenue away from the newspapers, many dailies dropped their radio sections. Publishers then began to pressure the press associations not to sell their services to stations not newspaper-owned.

The spearhead of their movement was the radio committee of the American Newspaper Publishers Association. Its militant chairman was Ed Harris, publisher of the Richmond, Indiana, *Palladium*. It seems ironic now that this small-town publisher could, and did, obstruct radio-news progress for so many years.

A weird series of events concerning the 1932 election greatly enhanced the influence of this committee. Radio had broadcast election results since 1920, but mostly in short bulletins. This year CBS decided to cancel its regular evening programs and concentrate on the election. A contract for such coverage was signed with the United Press. But a few days before the election the United Press decided to abrogate the contract; there had been too much pressure from its main source of revenue, the publishers.

The Associated Press, envious of the United Press, and not knowing they had canceled, offered its service free, with appropriate credits. So did William Randolph Hearst's International News Service. The newspaper publishers roared into action, cracked their long green money whip, and the AP, UP, and INS withdrew all service to broadcasters except under very special conditions.

This was not a mortal blow in 1933, since radio still had few regularly scheduled news programs. The networks offered news mostly through commentators such as Lowell Thomas, Boake Carter, Frederic William Wile, Kaltenborn, and Edwin C. Hill. These broadcasters, all experienced newspapermen, got their information from reading the newspapers and updating their stories by personal phone calls or telegrams.

In September of 1933 radio took a giant step forward with the formation of the Columbia News Service, a news-gathering organization for CBS only.

Edward Klauber, formerly an executive of *The New York Times*, now operating vice-president of CBS, brought Paul White, night news editor of the United Press and a brilliant graduate of the Missouri School of Journalism, to CBS in 1932 to head its publicity and special-events department. Klauber, news-oriented, was a strong supporter for more and better news in broadcasting.

At this propitious time the advertising manager of

General Mills in Minneapolis offered CBS a long-term news-sponsorship contract if the network would set up a news-gathering agency. CBS did so in September of 1933 under White's able direction.

CBS purchased the Dow Jones ticker service which gave comprehensive financial news, the Exchange Telegraph, a British agency for international coverage, and immediately established news bureaus in Washington, New York, Chicago, and Los Angeles. These bureaus, mostly staffed by former United Press men, who were old hands at operating on a tight budget and setting up stringers (part-time correspondents) in major cities.

In those days the AP had exclusive rights to all news published in its member papers. If a staffer on such a paper attempted to act as local man for the UP or INS, he was promptly fired. The men selected by White were experienced scroungers, and in a few weeks CBS had a remarkably good news service, and the network was broadcasting three daily newscasts, a noontime news program directed toward women and sponsored by General Mills, and two evening programs. In addition the service provided information for Boake Carter, H. V. Kaltenborn, and Edwin C. Hill.

The nerve center of the Columbia News Service was New York, where White had cleverly mixed veterans with eager young reporters. Among these were Ed Angly, a veteran overseas correspondent of the *Herald Tribune,* and Herbert Moore of the London Office of the United Press; Dixon Stewart and Sandy Kline of the UP's New York office; and Florence Conley, a smiling, aggressive young Irish girl from the *Journal-American.*

In that cold brisk autumn of 1933 there were no union

restrictions on working time or effort. The small New York staff worked six days, often ten or twelve hours at a stretch for what today seems like a pittance. I made $35 a week. We liked it, though, for it was a fascinating time to be a reporter.

Roosevelt was in the White House; and the country was regaining its confidence, and beginning to believe it could lick the depression. General Hugh Johnson was often in New York signing new NRA codes; Mrs. Roosevelt was emerging as a definite personality; Soviet Russia had just been recognized; there was a big championship prizefight looming between clowning Maxie Baer and the giant Primo Carnero from Italy; scavenger hunts were the rage, and Elsa Maxwell ran a big one at the Waldorf for charity.

I would often get up at 5:00 A.M., board a Coast Guard cutter, and meet an incoming liner to interview celebrities, be back at the office by noon for a couple of other assignments, and then cover a banquet or political rally at night.

Paul White, then about thirty, had a contagious enthusiasm about radio news. Paul had a sixth sense on story development, a skill that served him well in later years as he built CBS's famous worldwide news organization. He contributed as much as any man to news broadcasting as it is today.

First of all, White had definite ideas about style for radio. Most of his men were press-association trained, and used the "inverted pyramid" type of lead . . . or get those five *W*'s—who, where, what, when, and why—into the first sentence. This was ponderous and difficult for a listener to follow. If you miss a fact in the first sentence in a newspaper, you can reread it, but not so on radio. White encouraged us to develop a light, more conversational feature style of writing.

Radio's Finest Hour

Florence Conley scored the service's greatest triumph. She finagled her way past the heavily guarded front door of the Doris Duke mansion and got an exclusive interview with the "richest girl in the world" on her twenty-first birthday. We were delighted when the New York *Journal* asked for a copy of the interview, and printed it on Page One with full credit to the infant Columbia News Service.

Though I was fortunate enough to cover such major stories as the splendid Waldorf banquet for the new Russian Ambassador, Maxim Litvinov, several Roosevelt press conferences at his mother's town house in the East Sixties, interviews with Mrs. Roosevelt, General Johnson, and many stage and movie stars, the assignment I remember best was the first graduating class of the New York Bartenders Institute. Repeal was official in December of that year, and a new generation of bartenders had to be trained.

This was strictly a press agent's yarn, but because White thought it might be fun, I was asked to be one of the judges. A dozen young men in gleaming white jackets were standing behind a long mahogany bar. My job was to ask for any mixed drink I wanted, taste and evaluate. Well, after working myself through Manhattans, Martinis, Whisky Sours, Old-Fashioneds, Orange Blossoms, Ward Eights, and Bronxes, my judicial sense was less than objective. Then I was persuaded to sample a new creation enticingly called a Baby's Tit. This concoction, I discovered later, consisted of equal parts of cognac and crème d'violet topped with rum-flavored white cream and a big red cherry.

Never have I experienced such tortures of the dammed as I did the next day. I thought I might die, and was terribly unhappy that I didn't.

*   *   *

It Sounds Impossible

Soon, small-town dailies, who found the cost of their press services very high, requested permission to transcribe and print the CBS material. There were other papers who used the material without permission. CBS decided *not* to sell the Columbia News Service, but this did not satisfy the publishers.

The newspaper publishers increased their activity against radio. Program listings were dropped by scores of papers. The CBS Publicity Department claimed there was an unofficial boycott of CBS network-program news. Rumors were a dime a dozen. NBC and CBS would jointly underwrite a radio press service. Columbia News would be separated from the network and would be financed by a Wall Street group. CBS would continue regardless of pressure—but they were just rumors.

A week before Christmas, Paul White regretfully told his staff the service would be discontinued shortly after the first of the year. In January of 1934 a peace conference was held between the publishers and the broadcasters—and finally a most unsatisfactory peace for radio was made.

News was restored to radio through a strange organization called the Press-Radio Bureau. CBS and NBC paid the cost of this operation, and the three press services donated their news. CBS completely disbanded the Columbia News Service on March 1, 1934. The Press-Radio Bureau supplied two five-minute news summaries daily. The morning report could not be broadcast until after 9:30 A.M., the evening one after 9:00 P.M. The news could not be sponsored. Radio networks could give their audience news as a public service, but not until after the morning and evening editions were on the street.

The solution was about as stupid as Munich and lasted

about as long. First, the networks decided that Kalten-born, Lowell Thomas, Winchell, and company were not newscasters but "commentators" and that their programs could be sold.

Individual radio stations were not a party to the agreement, and resented the restrictions. They soon became clients of two independent radio news-gathering organizations: Transradio Press Service, Inc., which was begun by Herb Moore and Dixon Stewart of the Columbia News Service, and a regional service which was begun by John Shepard of the Yankee Network.

James Barrett, former city editor of the New York *World,* and a most capable newspaperman, was editor of the Press-Radio Bureau. He liberalized the bureau to try to meet the competition. News could now be broadcast at 8:00 A.M. and 6:00 P.M. The term in the agreement "transcendental importance" was given the most liberal interpretation, and the networks were given a much more comprehensive news service. But it was too late. Transradio became a national organization. It even numbered a few small dailies among its clients. The UP and INS realized they were protecting a competitor as well as losing potential revenue.

In 1935 INS removed all restrictions and began to sell its reports both to radio stations and to the networks. The UP followed a month later. The AP, which is a nonprofit organization controlled by member newspapers, did not fall in line until 1941.

Now that the services of the INS and the UP were available, both the networks and the individual stations quickly laid the solid foundation for news as it is presented today on radio and TV.

It Sounds Impossible

The networks expanded their foreign coverage. At the time of King Edward's abdication, it seemed that as many programs were originating from London as from New York. In 1938 the first multiple-news pickup from European capitals was begun by CBS. Bob Trout was in New York, William L. Shirer in London, Pierre Huss in Berlin, Edgar Mowrer in Paris, Edward R. Murrow in Vienna, and Senator Lewis B. Schwellenbach in Washington. Thus a new concept in news coverage came into being with Europe, and later the Pacific, as close as the nearest radio receiver.

The Press-Radio Bureau folded in 1938. The networks and the stations began organizing their own newsrooms and establishing news bureaus in major cities around the globe in preparation for what then appeared inevitable—World War II.

Promises,
Promises, Promises

F o r better or worse, radio has brought drastic changes in the American scene in four decades. Many observers believe that its impact has been the sharpest, the most decisive in the field of national politics.

Gone forever are the colorful torchlight parades, the elaborate coast-to-coast election trains with "whistle stop" talks from the back platform, the hundreds of speeches by party henchmen at schools, churches, and on the courthouse steps.

Campaigns are less dramatic and less entertaining, but the voter is certainly better informed on the issues of the day. First radio, and now radio and television together are partly responsible, though the credit must go to the politician himself. Campaigners were really the first to sense that radio was a revolutionary new medium of person-to-person communication. While singers, actors, and comedians were reluctant to appear on radio, the clergy feared it would reduce church attendance, and sport promoters, the gate receipts, and the educators termed it an "interesting gadget," the politicians sensed the potential power of the microphone, and embraced it with alacrity and affection.

At first radio was simply used to extend the audience of an existing political event. If a candidate made a speech, held a political rally, or dedicated a monument or a dam, a microphone would appear on the stand, and the happenings would be broadcast. There was no attempt to develop special skills for radio or any great understanding of its persuasive powers.

Then came Franklin D. Roosevelt and 1932.

While still Governor of New York, Mr. Roosevelt wrote: "Time after time in meeting legislative opposition, I have taken the issue directly to the voters by radio, and invariably I have met a most heartening response. Amid many developments of civilization which lead away from direct government by the people, the radio is one which tends on the other hand to restore contacts between the masses and their chosen leaders."

FDR and his "fireside chats," specially designed for the radio audience, saw broadcasting become a powerful arm of the government. And so it remained through the uncertain 1930's and the crucial war years. Then Madison Avenue got into the act in 1952, and used both radio and TV actually to "sell" a candidate to the American people. Minute commercials, jingles, ten-second spots, endorsements, and so on . . . all the "hard sell" techniques were used for Dwight D. Eisenhower.

The great debates, eight years later, between Nixon and Kennedy, another new technique, brought doubt and fear to the politician. Most of them believed that Nixon lost the election because of his appearances with his younger opponent. It's interesting to note that Governor Nelson A. Rockefeller, in his campaign for reelection in 1962, refused to debate his Democratic opponent, Robert M. Morgenthau.

Before analyzing in detail some of the future basic problems that will confront both the candidates and the radio-TV industry, let's quickly review broadcasting's amazing political history. It began of course, in November of 1920, when KDKA broadcast the Harding-Cox election returns.

Then a politico named Bill A. Magee, running for Mayor of Pittsburgh, used the facilities of KDKA for a campaign speech. Less than a year later, in June of 1921, a President of the United States talked to the American people for the first time on radio. Warren G. Harding, on a cross-country tour to the West Coast, scheduled a major talk in St. Louis on the problem of America's participation in the World Court. KSD, St. Louis, got permission to broadcast. WEAF (New York) announced it would carry President Harding's speech, if possible. For ten days and nights engineers worked to perfect the circuits necessary to transmit Harding's words over a thousand miles of telephone lines for a simultaneous broadcast by the New York station. The experiment was a great success.

The St. Louis Chamber of Commerce requested other radio stations to remain silent as a courtesy to the President of the United States while KSD and WEAF were airing his speech, and they did.

A few minutes after the speech, the President and the two stations received hundreds of telephone calls and telegrams reporting "perfect reception," and expressing appreciation of this service.

That same year, WGY, Schenectady, broadcast the inaugural ceremonies of Governor Alfred E. Smith at Albany; David Lloyd George of England was heard over WEAF; and former President Wilson, in his only public address after leaving the White House, was heard over a three-station hookup (WEAF, New York; WCAF, Washington; and WJAR, Providence).

Then came the opening of Congress by WRC, Washington, and President Calvin Coolidge's memorial speech to Warren G. Harding (WEAF, New York).

Probably radio's most famous voice, that of Franklin D. Roosevelt, was heard for the first time in 1923. He spoke over WJZ, New York, under the auspices of the Democratic National Committee, on "Why Waste Your Vote?"

The next year, 1924, came the first of the national conventions, long a colorful and fascinating feature, first on radio and now on television.

WGN (of the Chicago *Tribune*) persuaded the Republicans and the Democrats, without much difficulty, that such important events deserved national coverage. A network of sixteen stations in twelve cities brought to millions of avid listeners the antics of the GOP in Cleveland, and those of the Democrats in Madison Square Garden, New York.

Graham McNamee was at the microphone at both conventions. However, it was the Democratic Convention, deadlocked for fifteen long days between William Jennings Bryan and William Gibbs McAdoo, that made "Mac" a national figure and added a catchphrase to the language, "Alabama casts twenty-four votes for Underwood."

Promises, Promises, Promises

Former Governor James Brandon, chairman of his state's delegation, perfected a mixture of southern drawl and the clarion call of a coon hunter. "Alabama," he would shout, with a long dramatic pause, "casts twenty-four votes for Underwoo-ood." This was heard over one hundred times on the radio—and after about the tenth ballot, the fifteen thousand people in the Garden would join Brandon, and roar "Alabamaaa casts twenty-fouah votes for Underwoo-oo-od." It rolled and echoed among the iron rafters of the auditorium and around the nation by radio.

The Democrats finally compromised on John W. Davis and Governor Charles Bryan. Calvin Coolidge and Charles G. Dawes had been selected as the GOP standard bearers in an orderly and dull Cleveland Convention. However, the 1924 election became known as radio's first national election. Both parties realized that by radio they could talk directly to millions of potential voters throughout the country. On election eve, the final campaign speeches were carried on a network of twenty-seven stations, with the West added for the first time—Denver, Seattle, Portland, San Francisco, and Los Angeles.

McNamee liked to reminisce about this convention: "I worked sixteen hours a day for over two weeks—and I lost a lot of weight even though I lived on sandwiches and soda pop. God, how I hate sandwiches! I hope I never eat another one as long as I live."

And as far as anyone knows, he didn't.

Mac loved to imitate old Jim Brandon with his train dispatcher's delivery of "Alabama casts twenty-four votes for Underwood." His attempts to do a southern accent were mildly ridiculous, but great fun to hear.

In just ten years radio had become an accepted part of

the American political scene, at local, state, and national elections. In 1932 radio proved beyond question its tremendous influence.

In this election the majority of the newspapers opposed Mr. Roosevelt. A talented natural speaker, and a firm believer in radio, Mr. Roosevelt discussed the campaign issues in a relaxed, friendly manner with the voters, and won a landslide victory over Herbert Hoover.

It is true that in this election, more than in any other, Mr. Roosevelt traveled to every section of the United States. This was planned strategy; he was intent on presenting the voters with a dynamic image of energy and decision. He felt also that such a campaign would dispel the many rumors and half-truths about his physical condition. But wherever he went there was a microphone; and his speeches were broadcast to the nation.

The new President's inaugural address of March, 1933, convinced FDR and his "brain trust" that radio was far too important to be put away in mothballs and used only in election years. This great speech was the forerunner of the fireside chats that Mr. Roosevelt used so effectively during his years in the White House.

March 4, 1933, was a dull gray day in Washington, the overcast skies punctuated with gusts of rain. The banks of the nation had locked their doors. One out of every four workers was jobless. Factories were silent, stores almost deserted, and hunger marchers paraded the streets of New York and Chicago. Thousands of homeless, half-starved children roamed the countryside. Americans were afraid, desperate, almost without hope.

After being sworn in as President on the Roosevelt family Bible, FDR stood, bareheaded and stern, before the thousands of people who had gathered on the grounds of the Capitol. Across the country millions clustered around their radio sets.

The new President, in ringing tones, said: "This is a day of national consecration . . ." and then, a few moments later, "Let me assert my firm belief that *the only thing we have to fear is fear itself,* nameless, unreasoning, unjustified terror which paralyzes needed efforts to convert retreat into advance."

FDR went on: "This nation asks for action, and action now . . . we must act and act quickly. We must move as a trained and loyal army willing to sacrifice for the good of common discipline, because without such discipline no progress is made, no leadership becomes effective." He concluded with: "The people of the United States have not failed. They have asked for discipline and direction under leadership. They have made me the present instrument of their wishes. In the spirit of the gift I take it."

As one commentator said: "In Washington the weather remained cold and gray. Across the land the fog began to lift."

And across the nation the people responded. Nearly half a million of his radio listeners wrote letters of praise, encouragement, and approval. "It was the finest thing this side of heaven," said one letter.

Certainly this direct communication with the people was too useful to discard. In his famous "fireside chats" (named by Harry Butcher of CBS, Washington), the President went directly to the country and explained in simple, effective terms the complex problems of government. FDR made eight fireside chats in his first term, and six in 1933 and 1934.

It Sounds Impossible

FDR insisted that these chats be written in simple, conversational style. He liked to think of himself at ease in his own living room, having a friendly and frank talk with a few neighbors. He certainly conveyed that impression to his radio audience.

On the night of such broadcasts the President was wheeled into the diplomatic reception room on the ground floor of the White House. He sat at a desk, waved at a few friends, wisecracked with the radio announcers and engineers, and often borrowed a light for the cigarette in his long holder. He would then open a black leather loose-leaf notebook containing his speech, borrow a stopwatch, and open "on cue" with his inimitable "My Friends." (Even the President of the United States had to broadcast live in those days, so insistent were the networks against any prerecorded material.)

The President spoke in a relaxed tone at about one hundred words a minute. When it was over, he'd ask everyone present, "How'd it go?" for he liked praise. Then he smiled, waved good night to everyone, and was wheeled upstairs. As *Variety* said, "He was truly a great showman and the Barrymore of the White House."

Again in 1936 it was partly President Roosevelt's skillful use of radio that gave him a landslide victory over Governor Alfred E. Landon of Kansas.

This was a strange election in many ways. Opposed to FDR were such ill-assorted characters as Father Coughlin, Governor Eugene Talmadge of Georgia, his old friend "Al" Smith, Gerald K. Smith, the American Liberty League (financed by rich industrialists like the Du Ponts and John Raskob of General Motors), the conservative GOP party headed by Herbert Hoover, and a majority of the big-city daily newspapers.

Promises, Promises, Promises

Roosevelt's main fear concerning this election was the press. By direct communication with the people by radio, FDR somehow made them understand, and resent, the attitude of the newspapers. During a great demonstration for the President in Chicago, the crowd shouted, "To hell with the *Tribune!*" . . . "Down with the *Tribune!*" Thomas Stokes, a Washington columnist, wrote: "These people no longer had any respect for the press or confidence in it. The press had finally overreached itself."

The issue became a simple one—Roosevelt. The people were overwhelmingly for him. He carried every state except Maine and Vermont, and won the greatest victory in presidential history.

In this election the American Liberty League bought a few isolated radio commercials asking support for Landon, and the Republican National Committee attempted to use a Madison Avenue approach on radio.

The Committee prepared a series of radio spots that presented the case against the New Deal in soap-opera terms:

MARRIAGE LICENSE CLERK: Now what do you intend to do about the national debt?

PROSPECTIVE BRIDEGROOM: National debt . . . Me?

CLERK: You are going to establish a family, and as head of an American family you will shoulder a debt of more than $1017.26 . . . and it's growing every day. Do you still want to get married?

GROOM: You . . . er . . . er . . . er . . . I. What do you say, Mary?

MARY: Maybe . . . maybe . . . we'd better talk it over first, John. All those Debts. When we thought we didn't owe anybody in the world.

JOHN: Somebody is giving us a dirty deal. It's a lowdown mean trick.

It Sounds Impossible

VOICE OF DOOM (OVER MUSIC): And the debts like the sins of the fathers shall be visited upon the children, aye, even unto the third and fourth generation.

To their credit, both NBC and CBS refused this advertising. An NBC spokesman said, "It would place the discussion of vital political and national issues on the basis of dramatic license rather than upon the basis of responsibility for stated fact or opinion."

Many industry leaders today deeply regret that this policy was changed, and believe that broadcasting lost tremendous prestige when it allowed Madison Avenue to participate in elections.

Again in 1940, when FDR defied tradition, and ran for a third term against Wendell Willkie, the newspapers were almost solidly against him. *Variety* said:

Unquestionably the biggest figure in all show business of 1940 was FDR, whose radio rating hit a new high with a Crossley rating of 38.7. His election for a third term demonstrated as nothing else could, the power of American radio. More than a political contest, the 1940 election was a battle between newspapers and radio to test which medium exercised the greatest influence on the American public. When the papers lined up almost 90 percent solidly against the third term, Roosevelt took his case to the people by the airwaves. Newspapers denied that the victory had been a clear cut one, claiming that the Roosevelt voice and personality was as much of a factor in the victory as the medium of radio.

One thing was sure, though, and that was that radio had come of age and had equal status with, if not greater status than, the press. It was to be used extensively in all future political campaigns, and the networks were committed to provide extensive and complete coverage of the national political conventions.

On April 13, 1945, millions were plunged into grief by the sad tidings brought to a stunned world by radio that FDR was dead. It was hard indeed to accept the fact that the warm radio voice with its heartening "My friends" would speak no more.

Out of respect and appreciation for the President, radio eliminated all commercials and canceled many programs that were unsuited to the mood of its listeners. And somehow it was fitting that radio should broadcast his funeral with simple dignity to the world.

Radio reached another milestone of importance in 1945 when President Harry Truman dedicated a new radio news gallery in the Senate wing of the Capitol.

"Radio," said the President, "has made the United States one great auditorium. In no other way can men instantly talk to all of this nation's millions. To safeguard our basic democratic principles, radio must be utilized to its fullest extent. Then the ancient demagogues of the old world will find no place in our way of life."

Though broadcasters agree with President Truman that radio and TV must "be utilized to its fullest extent" in the political field, they face two basic problems that have no quick and easy solutions. One is the desirability of commercial advertising by candidates; the other, the perplexing question of "equal time" for all candidates under Section 315 of the Federal Communications Act of 1934.

Radio spot announcements have been in limited use in national elections since 1936. They were mostly one-voice commercials, extolling the virtues of the candidate, rather dull, and generally used in markets where formal speeches were broadcast at low audience levels.

In 1948, BBD&O suggested that a large part of the GOP campaign budget be devoted to radio and TV spots. They would feature the candidate, use the latest advertising techniques, and to some extent replace the broadcast campaign speech. Thomas E. Dewey, the Republican standard bearer, said No, and, according to one Madison Avenue pundit, lost the election because of this decision.

In 1952 two New York ad-agency executives, Al Hollender of the Grey Agency and Rosser Reeves of Ted Bates & Company, are credited with persuading General Eisenhower and his brother Milton that "spots" should be used.

They stressed three basic points: the low cost per thousand of homes reached; the fact that, unlike speeches, spots would reach people not prejudiced in favor of the candidate or particularly interested in or knowledgeable about politics; and third, that propaganda could be concentrated in critical pivotal states or even cities.

The GOP spent several million dollars on radio and TV spots, and most of them went about like this:

ANNOUNCER (March of Time voice): *Eisenhower Answers the Nation!*

ORDINARY CITIZEN: Mr. Eisenhower [never "General," as this was considered a negative symbol], what about all this high cost of living?

EISENHOWER: You know, my wife, Mamie, worries about the same thing. I tell her it's our job to change all that on November 4th.

Using this same technique, Eisenhower covered what the experts considered the basic issues of the campaign;

the Korean War, corruption in Washington, taxes (always), and the high cost of living.

While it's generally conceded (except for Reeves, who contended Stevenson could have been elected if he had used spots correctly) that this type of radio and TV commercial was a minor factor in "Ike's" campaign, it could be vital in a very close election.

The common objection to advertising in politics is that it oversimplifies. This is fine in selling a standard brand, for the customer simply doesn't buy the product again unless he likes it. He doesn't have this option with a candidate without waiting four years.

When this technique of oversimplification is applied to political issues, it often misinforms, creates undesirable emotions, and distorts facts. It's obvious that if a close election were decided by such advertising, it would hardly be the democratic ideal of an informed and responsible people making their own decisions. Certainly democracy does not benefit by emotional slogans presenting simplified and one-sided views of complicated affairs of state.

And this is the headache that faces the responsible broadcaster. Should he refuse to accept such advertising, and on what grounds? Though it's hardly "in the public interest," is this a competent, legal reason for declining an order from a reputable advertising agency? Can he refuse to broadcast political advertising and still live up to his "fairness and balance" obligations? The National Association of Broadcasters has no firm position on this issue, and neither does a vast majority of radio and TV station operators.

A modification of Section 315, the "equal time clause," would certainly help clarify the issue of political advertising.

It Sounds Impossible

This section states that a broadcaster who gives or sells time to a political candidate must be prepared to give or sell equal time to any and every legally qualified rival candidate.

In the summer of 1960 the Congress temporarily suspended the equal-time provisions in the presidential race only, and this made possible the now famous Nixon-Kennedy debates.

Walter Lippmann said in September of 1960: "The TV debate was a bold innovation which is bound to be carried forward into future campaigns and could not now be abandoned. From now on it will be impossible for any candidate for any important elective office to avoid this kind of confrontation with his opponent."

But this remains to be seen. In the off-year elections of 1962 there was no suspension of Section 315, and once again broadcasters who wanted to give the American public the information it wanted and needed were thwarted. *Broadcasting Magazine* said that they were "confused, bothered and bewildered," in trying to interpret and enforce this amendment.

Certainly this law should be repealed or modified before the 1964 elections. Radio and television should have the right to exercise their own news judgment, and invited candidates should be able to meet in debate or joint discussion.

Dr. Frank Stanton, President of the Columbia Broadcasting System, and long an ardent advocate of modification of Section 315, said recently:

Indeed, the debate is the most effective campaign device for fully enlightening voters about the views and capabilities of rival candidates. It is a ludicrous and wasteful anachronism that what was permitted over a century ago in great public meetings, is forbidden now in what, through television and radio, would be nothing less than public meetings made infinitely greater by admitting all citizens. We cannot hope to press forward the improvement of the essential democratic machinery if—instead of taking advantage of the technical achievements of our age—we become victims of changes that have made the political methods of yesterday useless.

It is not the United States that is on trial before the world today. It is the survival of the democratic idea, the workability of democracy, in an age of relentless pressures. We *must* make democracy work. All our exhortations, all our negotiations, all our policies and actions are useless if democracy here at home does not work.

We need to use, now and at all levels of self-government, every new instrument this modern age has put at our command to make democracy work . . . and work well. This is our opportunity, our obligation, our necessity.

Most broadcasters would willingly accept this obligation, if the Congress will give them the opportunity.

CHAPTER 19

How Are Ya?
How Are Ya?

B Y   T H E time the radio industry had developed program experts to figure out what the public wanted, the radio audience was making up its own quiet mind what it would and would not listen to. Listeners were also showing definite tendencies toward fickleness and selectivity.

In the latter part of the thirties radio had developed not a single new runaway hit to captivate the public. While "Amos 'n' Andy" and Fibber McGee were still going strong, and while Bob Hope and Bing Crosby were putting on top shows with high ratings and garnering much appreciation, the national audience hadn't had a really bright new star in a half-dozen years.

Then Arthur Godfrey happened. Godfrey was one of the very few "true radio" performers. He had begun in the medium and had had nothing to do with any other.

Godfrey came into the national picture along with the

1940's, and for him he couldn't have picked a better time to be a star. His personality fit the times in that America was ready for an easygoing, devil-may-care, resist-authority-but-love-my-country, big-brother or uncle image. World War II was on, and what with the Armed Forces looking toward an eventual strength of twelve million men, with rationing, war plants, war bonds, sleepless nights and worry, the country was ready for this pleasant guy with the deep laugh.

Ten years after his first daytime network show, "Arthur Godfrey Time" on CBS—a morning affair that began as a sustainer and was later sponsored by Chesterfield cigarettes—Godfrey had become a very controversial entertainer. But not in the way that any other entertainer was ever controversial. He had never been tinged with any political gossip, been involved in any scandal concerning liquor or women, hit a photographer, or sued for slander. If anything, Godfrey was probably victimized by the press. Although New York newspapers protest their innocence in the handling of stories, a retrospective look at the headlines of 1953 will bear out what a tornado in a teacup the press can create—not without plenty of help from the actor's "friend"—the press agent.

Godfrey had fired a few of the entertainers on his program—starting with an Italian boy named Julius La Rosa whom Godfrey had met aboard an aircraft carrier in Pensacola, Florida, in 1951. It was the case of a big star giving a big break to an unknown sailor with a mildly pleasant voice. Godfrey presented La Rosa on his show a few times, and then, on the air one morning, publicly asked the young singer if he'd like to become a regular member of the Little Godfreys, as he called his cast. La Rosa wept

213

with joy. Everybody loved Godfrey and everybody loved La Rosa. In the nearly two years that followed, La Rosa developed from an awkward kid into a pretty fair entertainer. In May of 1953, Godfrey entered the hospital for a very serious hip operation. He was at the peak of his popularity. The day he went in for surgery many papers had his picture on their front pages, with captions reading: "GOOD LUCK, RED!" "BRING THAT SMILE BACK SOON, ARTHUR!" "GOD BLESS YOU, GODFREY!"

And when he came back to his show after three months, the press was glad to see him. The radio section of one big paper ran a banner head: "SEEMS LIKE OLD TIMES; ARTHUR'S BACK."

When Godfrey returned, the Little Godfreys had changed. As Godfrey put it, "I didn't have a cast anymore. I had a galaxy of stars."

La Rosa was making $2,000 and $3,000 a show for a personal appearance while Godfrey was paying him a paltry $1,000 a week for the show that made him a valuable property.

One day Godfrey got a letter telling him that in the future, if he wanted to talk to La Rosa, to see his lawyer.

Godfrey, after some thought and discussion with his friends and associates at CBS, decided to buy out La Rosa's contract. He then dismissed him the way he hired him—on the air. Considering what happened then, it wasn't necessarily the smartest thing Godfrey ever did. A soap opera broke loose in the newspapers:

FIRING UNFAIR SAYS LA ROSA IN TEARS

JULIUS RISES IN DEFENSE OF GODFREY GIRL SINGER

JAN DAVIS SEES SELF NEXT TO GO

How Are Ya'? How Are Ya'?

CBS crawled with reporters wanting stories—any kind of story to get on the Godfrey-is-a-mean-man bandwagon. The morning papers and the evening papers carried front-page stories for days.

A situation like this can happen only to a famous man. Otherwise it wouldn't be news. The setup has to be right, too.

In the summer of 1959, Perry Como, a superb entertainer and good show-business administrator, ordered the replacement of nearly all the Ray Charles Singers and the Louis DePron dancers so that his television show would present fresh new voices and faces to the public the following fall. The kids on the unemployment lines didn't chide or berate Como for this action. Not a word was said in the press. Big shows change personnel constantly. It's for the good of the show—because every producer and star must constantly remember how fickle the public is. Nothing is so deadly as a program that is getting stale. Shows with "families" are the most vulnerable to the wrath of certain sections of the audience when a "faithful friend" is removed.

The first "Arthur Godfrey Time" on radio and his CBS show today have virtually the same approach. The star is seated in an informal grouping around a few microphones in Columbia's Studio One. The cast is relaxed, jovial, and happy. They kid with one another—ad-lib little gags and puns—while the master runs things with the help of some carefully collected informational odds and ends plus an occasional sketch or setup gag provided by his writer, Bob Carman. The show plays as well today as it did in the forties, except that there is no studio audience present, and as a result Godfrey doesn't receive the long boff laughs he used to enjoy in the show's salad days. The cast laughs it up, however, in the hope of making the humor infectious at the home level.

The hail-fella-well-met Godfrey of the airshow is not the same Godfrey we see daily climb out of his chauffeur-driven Bentley. He walks with a cane but does not lean on it. He looks more like the vice-president type than like the grinning entertainer who started out as Ukulele Red. He has, believe it or not, a stately air about him. He nods good-naturedly to those in the lobby and chats with secretaries and mailboys who happen to be riding the same elevator with him. He arrives alone and leaves alone. Upon his departure in the early evening, it's not uncommon to see Neil, his driver, slip into the back seat while Godfrey takes the wheel of his car.

It is probable, over the years, that more people have wondered what Arthur Godfrey was really like than ever concerned themselves with Jack Paar, who used that line as a running gag for a long time.

Amazingly enough, it's difficult to get two sides to the Godfrey story. Even people who might dislike him seem to like him.

We ran into an old friend who had been with Godfrey for twelve years as his director, producer, and talent-getter. A week before we met for lunch, he had been fired by Godfrey with no immediate prospects for reemployment. He was a most capable man, but radio and TV in New York were tightening up, and there are no frantic calls out for producers or directors, no matter how well qualified. He looked unworried as he swung into the Berkshire 500 Club across from CBS. He still looked like

How Are Ya'? How Are Ya'?

Godfrey's producer—cashmere coat, graying hair, rapid gait, and a big smile.

During the first Martini we got right to the point.

"What do you think about Arthur Godfrey?"

There wasn't a second's hesitation.

"Arthur Godfrey is two different guys. I respect him. He's the world's greatest. There isn't anybody like him," the producer said.

"Who are these two people?" we asked.

"Well," he replied, "there's Godfrey the performer and Godfrey the man. When you get away from the performer, Godfrey is not a funny man. He is totally dedicated to his show's success. On stage you see him laughing and gagging around, but in his office he's all business."

Godfrey the performer. We recalled the days of his early television shows when, as host, he would involve himself in every conceivable situation. If it were a skating show he'd become Godfrey the skater . . . a circus show— Godfrey the acrobat. He'd master anything for a good show. He had played Broadway in the mid-forties—but we had heard that he turned down many motion picture offers. We wondered why.

We wondered why Godfrey had never played around with other media much—movies, the theater, nightclubs.

"Godfrey must be Godfrey," he told us. "He won't play a role. Maybe there was a time when he could, before all this happened to him. Maybe there was a time when he could have forgotten Godfrey and been somebody else in a situation. But not now. As soon as he plays a part, he's no good. That's why we never gave him sketches to do—the way other comics worked. A contrived character and Arthur just don't mix."

It Sounds Impossible

What our friend did not know was that at the time of our talk, Godfrey was considering a situation comedy series on TV.

We asked him why he felt Godfrey swept the nation in such a big way: Was it the big voice, the booming laugh, his singing, the talent he surrounded himself with—what?

"His angle," our friend answered. "His approach. His concept of his audience. Godfrey has a knack in front of a microphone of being able to talk to people at their own level."

This statement, which we had heard before, had always mystified us. When an entertainer talks to a listener "on the listener's own level," what is he doing? Is the star lowering himself to accomplish this? Is he being himself? Or, in some wild way, is he bettering his station? We asked the producer.

"Godfrey has the image of his audience as individuals. This individual is a plain person. An ordinary, average Joe. Godfrey knows what this is. You must remember, he'd been a deckhand, a door-to-door salesman, and even sold cemetery lots before he went on the air. He knows what 'plain' is. He knows what the inside of the average middle-income house looks like—and he doesn't need a gang of statisticians to tell him, either. A couple of million dollars hasn't changed the way he talks. On the air he's still the big ol' Peck's bad boy with orange hair and a uke."

Then he got on the subject of Godfrey's material. "I wouldn't suggest anything for his show that my mother-in-law wouldn't understand. The gags had to be easy, cute, funny—and Godfrey."

How Are Ya'? How Are Ya'?

"What about the people in his casts—Janette Davis, Bill Lawrence, the Chordettes, Lou Ann Simms, Julius La Rosa—the rest?" We laid it out. "Were they really talented? Were they star material?"

He answered simply: "They weren't the greatest performers, but they were people that other people could understand. We get back to that old thing 'association.' La Rosa could be the lucky kid down the block. A few were outstanding— a very few. The McGuire Sisters were different. They listened and they worked. That's the reason they're such great stars today. They were three very talented, good-looking kids who were audience pleasers because they were willing to work."

And what about the others? What was the reason for the firings?

"Simple," he said. "They just weren't good enough, and refused to cooperate. They'd trot out old material, and when Arthur asked them why they didn't learn something new, something fresh, the answer would most always be, 'I'm too busy.' This was never an acceptable answer for Arthur. And it wouldn't be to anyone who was paying these kids what he was paying them, and giving them daily coast-to-coast exposure that they couldn't buy.

"But especially with Arthur. He never lets up. This man never took a real honest-to-God vacation in all the years I worked for him. He was always figuring out something new. It shows in his work. Nobody, but nobody, can pick up the sticks the way he can. When he isn't there, by God, you miss him."

There were a few years when no one was on the coast-to-coast air more than Godfrey, and all his shows had top ratings. It was not uncommon to find his daily radio show

219

outstripping all competition, and his two nighttime television shows rating Number One and Two.

Like many fabulous careers, Godfrey's began with tragedy. In 1931 he suffered a serious injury in an automobile accident. The long period of convalescence that followed made a deep imprint on his personality, and incidentally on his whole approach to radio broadcasting.

In his hospital bed, Godfrey spent a great deal of time listening to the radio, and came to realize that this could be—but wasn't—a truly intimate medium. He realized that announcers and performers in front of microphones were not talking—they were reading, and therefore convincing no one.

"I recalled my experiences as a house-to-house salesman, and I remember that even where there was an urgent need for the product I was selling, I couldn't make a sale unless I first sold my customer on myself. If the lady of the house had no confidence in me, she wouldn't even listen to me," said Godfrey.

"Radio . . . was nothing but door-to-door selling. I wouldn't knock on some woman's door, and when she opened it, bellow: 'Good Morning, ladies and gentlemen. This is Arthur Godfrey speaking!' She'd slam it in my face and phone for the cops!"

And so when Godfrey returned to broadcasting, listeners heard, for the first time, the casual, unhurried speech . . . the ruminating, hesitant pace . . . the purring growl that has since "opened the doors" to millions of American homes.

Not every ex-employee shares our friend's respect for Godfrey, but no boss ever ran up a perfect score. One of

How Are Ya'? How Are Ya'?

Godfrey's former writers shared a cup of cheer with us, and drew an analogy with a barroom flavor.

"Fame is pretty intoxicating stuff," he said, "and only certain people can take it. When you put a bottle of good whiskey on the table in front of a man, the amount of liquor he drinks is a measure of breeding. There are connoisseurs and alcoholics. The position into which Godfrey was catapulted was too much for him. He got drunk on fame."

True or not, Godfrey set some sensational records.

Godfrey's programs have brought millions upon millions of dollars into the CBS coffers, and his sponsorship record is more striking in view of the limitations he puts on accounts. It is true that he will not accept for sponsorship any product that he, personally, is not satisfied with. Last year he turned down five products.

Advertisers who sell products competitive to the over eighty products he now sells are unacceptable.

If Godfrey stops advertising a product, he will not consider switching to a competing brand for months— sometimes years—afterward.

It's Godfrey's unique selling technique that is responsible for his advertising effectiveness. The fact that he puts everything he's got into everything he does makes him a great salesman.

Variety called Godfrey "one of the major phenomena of his era. A one-man industry."

Godfrey has an earthiness, an independence, and an enthusiasm that register. One day in Washington, where he was a sensation as the city's top early-morning man, he suddenly remarked: "Ain't this the silliest thing? Here I am playing the 'William Tell Overture' at eight minutes

after seven when everyone wants a little peace and quiet."
Then he proceeded to smash the record. His fans loved it.
So he broke phonograph records on almost every broadcast. No one explained that there wouldn't be so much
record-breaking if the selection of music had been a little
better—it was Godfrey's gimmick, and that's what his
listeners loved.

Arthur Godfrey hasn't changed his air personality. The
only thing his fans have come to expect is the unexpected.

CHAPTER 20

The Fatal Fifties

Radio was dead: to begin with. There is no doubt whatever about that. The register of its burial was signed by the clergyman, the clerk, the undertaker, and the chief mourner. Scrooge signed it: and Scrooge's name was good upon the 'Change, for anything he chose to put his hands to. Old Radio was as dead as a door-nail.

Mind! I don't mean to say that I know, of my own knowledge, what there is particularly dead about a door-nail. I might have been inclined, myself, to regard a coffin-nail as the deadest piece of ironmongery in the trade. But the wisdom of our ancestors is in the simile; and my unhallowed hands shall not disturb it, or the Country's done for. You will therefore permit me to repeat, emphatically, that radio was as dead as a door-nail.

—Courtesy of Charles Dickens

I n 1950, television, though in only 8 percent of American homes, seemed to have killed its big brother—radio. The reasons given are both numerous and ingenious, and none are quite satisfactory.

In analyzing the almost fantastic decline in radio's

importance during the past decade, let's glance at the program schedules of January, 1950.

In the morning the Breakfast Club on ABC and Arthur Godfrey on CBS were the two most popular programs on radio. Today, though far less dominating, these programs are still on radio, and maintain respectable ratings.

CBS scheduled daytime serials beginning at noon and running for three hours, which gave the network more than double the audience of any of its competitors. The bloc ran like this: "Wendy Warren," "Aunt Jenny," "Helen Trent," "Our Gal Sunday," "Big Sister," "Ma Perkins," "Young Dr. Malone," "The Guiding Light," "The Second Mrs. Burton," "Perry Mason," "This Is Nora Drake," "The Brighter Day," "Nona from Nowhere," "Hilltop House," and "House Party."

Then, exactly at 3:00 P.M., NBC moved into first place in audience size with "Life Can Be Beautiful," "Road to Life," "Pepper Young's Family," "Right to Happiness," "Backstage Wife," "Stella Dallas," "Lorenzo Jones," "Young Widder Brown," "When a Girl Marries," "Portia Faces Life," "Just Plain Bill," and "Front-Page Farrell."

In the early evening, news commentators Lowell Thomas, Fulton Lewis, Jr., Ed Murrow, Gabriel Heatter, Elmer Davis, and H. V. Kaltenborn dominated the ratings.

On a typical Monday night listeners heard "Inner Sanctum," "Arthur Godfrey's Talent Scouts," "Lux Radio Theatre," "My Friend Irma," or, if they preferred music, there were the "Voice of Firestone," "The Telephone Hour," and "Kate Smith Calls."

Tuesday was Mystery night on CBS, with "Mr. and Mrs. North," "Mystery Theatre," and "Escape"; comedy night on NBC, with "The Bob Hope Show," Fanny Brice as Baby Snooks, and "Fibber McGee and Molly." ABC offered discussion, with "Town Meeting of the Air."

The remainder of the week listeners could select among such programs as "Dr. I.Q.," "The Bing Crosby Show," "Break the Bank," "Mr. District Attorney," "Burns and Allen," "Blondie," "The Aldrich Family," "Screen Guild Theatre," "The Goldbergs," "Halls of Ivy," with Ronald Colman; Jimmy Durante, "Truth or Consequences," "Gangbusters," "Your Hit Parade," and "Hollywood Star Theatre."

Sunday was the big night with such perennial favorites as Jack Benny, Fred Allen, Edgar Bergen, Amos 'n' Andy, Red Skelton, and "Stop the Music."

Radio in 1950 offered tremendous program selection—comedy, drama, music, news, commentary, and discussion.

Today, with one or two exceptions, not a single program or personality listed above is on the air. There's not one soap opera or dramatic program, not one major comedy program or comic, and the only big music program left is the New York Philharmonic-Symphony which is still broadcast by CBS.

Lowell Thomas and Fulton Lewis, Jr., are the last of the commentators, and time is running out on Arthur Godfrey and Don McNeill's Breakfast Club.

The obvious answer to radio's decline and fall would be far superior television programs. But was it?

In that pivotal year of 1950 the ten most popular nighttime television programs were "Texaco Star Theatre," with Milton Berle; "The Goldbergs," "Toast of the Town," with Ed Sullivan; "Arthur Godfrey's Talent Scouts," "Studio One," "Godfrey and His Friends," "Suspense," "Lights Out," "Philco Playhouse," and "Fireside

It Sounds Impossible

Theatre." The daytime leaders were "Howdy Doody," "Captain Video," "Small Fry Club," "Lucky Pup," "Junior Frolics," "Kukla, Fran, and Ollie," "Camel News Caravan," "Western Features" (movies), "Children's Theatre," and "Mohawk Showroom."

Only Ed Sullivan and the 6:45 news program, now with another sponsor on NBC, have managed to stand the test of time. Remember, too, that in 1950 most screens were black until noon and even later. Then TV was offering such oddball programs as roller derbies, staged wrestling, boxing, and scores of gimmick programs that could be produced inexpensively.

Today it's hard to believe that such programming would cause the average American to plunk down $400 or $500 for a TV set, but television had caught the fancy of Americans much sooner than even the most optimistic researcher had predicted. The novelty factor was the miracle of pictures through the air, and the fact that most of it was dreadful was of no consequence.

In 1950 there were 3,375,000 TV sets in use; a year later, nearly 10,000,000; and by 1955 TV sets totaled 31,000,000. Today there are over 50,000,000 TV sets in the United States.

During this same period it would be natural to assume that radio sets were becoming as obsolete as the model-T Ford, but this was not so. In 1950 there were some 50,000,000 radio sets, nearly all in the home. Today there are over 100,000,000 radio sets in the home. True, they are not in the living room, but in the bedroom, kitchen, den, or workshop.

In addition, today there are 40,000,000 radio sets in automobiles. A car radio set today is as standard as a spare tire. There are also 10,000,000 sets in public places—restaurants, small shops, and filling stations, and an estimated another 10,000,000 transistor sets at the beach, the ballgame, picnics, or in the hands of teenagers as they stroll around the town. Today radio sets are outselling television two to one, and far more homes have radios than telephones, bathtubs, or refrigerators.

Why, then, the drastic decline in the quality of radio programming and its importance as a national advertising medium?

First, and most important, was the tremendous increase in the number of radio stations. In 1945 there were 943 licensed radio stations. Five years later there were over 2,000, and today there are well over 4,000 AM and FM stations in the United States. This tremendous increase led to what researchers term "fragmentation of the audience." What happened in New York is typical of major markets throughout the nation. In 1950 the three network stations, WNBC, WABC, and WCBS, had over 40 percent of the share of audience. Today they have about 20 percent share compared to 80 percent for the independents. Also, since 1950, within a radius of fifty miles of New York, over 25 new radio stations have begun operating. Even though these small stations count their audience in the thousands, they have all lured audience away from the "majors."

In 1950 the audience spent just about as much time with the radio as they did in front of the TV screen. A decade later the hours of viewing per TV home, according to the A. C. Neilsen Company, had risen to five hours daily while radio had dropped to two hours.

Faced with smaller audiences and amazing interest in television, it seems incredible today how little the networks, and the movies for that matter, did to meet this new competition.

There were abortive attempts at new big-time programming. NBC produced "The Big Show," an hour-long extravaganza on Sunday, with Tallulah Bankhead, Meredith Willson's orchestra, and big-name guest stars. But it was the same old variety-show format, and frequently was a bore. CBS tried several new variety musical programs, and ABC offered new giveaways and audience-participation programs. But it was the old story of too little and too late.

Radio in 1950 was fat, smug, self-satisfied, and very rich. Most programs had a high level of competence and an equally high level of sameness. To compete with the picture tube, radio badly needed the invigorating effect of a new production style for dramas and documentaries. It needed to develop new comedians and singers, writers and directors, and new program concepts.

It didn't. As advertisers deserted the big network radio shows, both money and creative people were becoming scarce. The control of TV had passed to the networks, the stations and the sponsors who had established the standards of radio broadcasting. They had a new toy now—an expensive, exciting, shining new medium. And when we consider all the criticism of broadcasting over the years by intellectuals, a fairly hostile press, and publicity-seeking politicians, this was a great vote of confidence by the American people.

The three major networks were sinking huge sums of money and most of their creative energies into the development of television. Because radio had to pay the bills for its potential destroyer, it couldn't, or wouldn't upset the *status quo* that kept the cash registers ringing; therefore, new concepts went begging.

The networks, through economic necessity, pushed their ablest executives into blueprinting the future for television. They couldn't afford to make many mistakes in programming: they were too expensive. They couldn't allow TV to grow like Topsy, as early network radio had done, or it would bankrupt them. Thus, the margin for experiment was much slimmer, and TV was built along the conventional, successful program lines that had been pretested for years by radio.

As radio profits were plowed into TV, it suffered from a slow but sure attrition during the fatal fifties. The exodus began with "Lux Radio Theatre." It was followed by "The Bob Hope Show"; then other comics like Martin and Lewis and Edgar Bergen followed. Jack Benny stayed around for several years, but his programs were not new. Old Benny shows were edited and rebroadcast. The half-hour dramas disappeared; Amos 'n' Andy became disc jockeys, and their offering the "The Amos 'n' Andy Music Hall." They used small bits from old comedy routines between records.

Show after show was canceled as sponsors quit radio and jumped into television with amazing speed, considering its size and its costs. Advertisers felt that television's integration of sight, sound, motion, and immediacy gave it a decided advantage over all other forms of advertising. Television became the Pied Piper of media, and advertisers fled radio and magazines in droves to get their products on the home screen. Television hogged the publicity spotlight as magazines and newspapers devoted millions of words to criticizing or praising this new electronic marvel.

It Sounds Impossible

Sponsors became "TV happy," and most advertising agencies urged their clients to jump into this new, wild wonderland for sales increases. To resist this television tidal wave might prove fatal—and in several cases did—to a good agency-client relationship.

Network radio licked its financial wounds and tried to compete with this new monster by reducing program costs and its rate structure for time sales. Neither was effective.

Many broadcasters today think that radio panicked in the fifties and made too few effective moves to compete with TV. They claim that radio men knew an animated picture was worth a thousand words and that sound could not compete in this field of entertainment; therefore comedy, variety, and drama had to die. Some feel that radio should have junked its existing programs immediately, instead of allowing them to die slowly, and substituted the type of news and informational programming that gives radio its vitality today.

But it's easy to be a Sunday quarterback. Perhaps only through trial and error could radio find its proper place in the broadcasting field, which it seems to have done today.

Radio's Worst Hour

BERT PARKS had just finished reading through the script in NBC's Studio 6-A. In the fifteen minutes before airtime, we began to talk about the shows he had emceed over the years—"The Camel Caravan," with Vaughn Monroe; "Stop the Music," "Break the Bank"—and the excitement these programs used to generate. He looked out into 6-A's auditorium. It was only a third filled, and at best would be only half filled by airtime despite the fact that the bands about to perform were Freddy Martin and Ray McKinley. Of course, we offered, this was 1957 not 1947. Things were different.

Bert smiled, and asked, "Did you ever get the feeling that the whole business is sliding into the lake?"

He was more right than kidding. Network radio was in pain. "Bert Parks' Bandstand," the last of the big music-variety shows, was sold out commercially, but everyone knew its days were numbered.

It would be another of the radio network music features no one would hear anymore.

It Sounds Impossible

The Panther Room of the Hotel Sherman, the "Cradle of Swing," was gone, and so were the big-band sounds that were broadcast from there. Never again would there be dance remotes from the Glen Island Casino featuring the music of Glenn Miller and his orchestra, with Tex Beneke, Paula Kelly, and the Modernaires. Dick Jurgens' band would never be heard from Chicago's Trianon again, nor would listeners ever spend another Saturday afternoon listening to the great bands of the land playing a "Matinee" at Frank Daly's Meadowbrook, "just off the Newark-Pompton Turnpike in Cedar Grove, New Jersey!"

The big variety shows were a thing of the past. Bert Parks had maintained some semblance of comedy on his show by keeping Arnold Stang and Pat Carroll around as "regulars" with frequent guest appearances by other people. The show sounded good. It was just that the networks and the public had had it.

NBC made three noteworthy passes at doing something about network programming. During the regime of Sylvester "Pat" Weaver, the network began the first of the new marathon programs called "Monitor." Starting on Friday night and continuing until Monday morning each weekend, NBC began the formidable task of throwing the entire broadcast entertainment book at the listener. "Monitor" microphones were everywhere—in a parade, at an amusement park, in a death cell of a prison, on the top of a mountain, and in a submarine. "Monitor," at the outset, was every special event ever conceived—and delivered on a nonstop basis. The sessions were highlighted with hard news, comedy spots, good music on records and, it seemed mostly, cutaways for local station commercials. "Monitor," under the direction of James Fleming, was a sock listener success, and for years it was a commercial success. Somewhere along the way the concept got lost and after five years or so the program settled down into a series of short commercial features loosely hooked together. The grand idea of two personalities on each segment of the show met the economic cutback ax. Where at first interviews with famous people were sometimes inspired, they later dragged into boredom as unqualified interviewers asked the same tired questions of movie stars, authors, and music personalities whose sole purpose in being on "Monitor" was to plug something—a movie, book, or record album.

The show that was forever "going places and doing things" was going fewer places and doing fewer things.

The first success of "Monitor" led programmers at NBC to believe that by wiping out the few remaining soap operas and stretching the same idea across the board, radio programming might be saved.

Mitchell Benson was named executive producer of a show called "Weekday." Mitch had a bigger book to throw. He reasoned that if the network gave a lady listener every conceivable thing she could want in the way of service, information, and entertainment, she would stick by her set. He hired Margaret Truman and Mike Wallace as the mainstays for the six-hour, five-day-a-week experiment. The communicators for the two hours from 12:00 noon to 2:00 P.M. were Martha Scott and Walter Kiernan.

"Weekday" offered everything. Each day a "star companion" was on hand for the full six hours. There were excellent little drama spots, a best-selling novel was serialized, music features included "Meredith Willson's Music Room" and backstage interviews on the eve of a Broadway opening. There were health and medical features, and cooking was covered. There was news and there were news features.

Most of all there were problems, almost all of them economic. NBC didn't pay for "star companions" like Eddie Fisher, Rosemary Clooney, Dennis Day, or Bob Hope. Each was on the show for the plugola—and generally the network promised to feature the star's recordings all through the day. The star wasn't "live." Generally he was interviewed by someone who never appeared on the show, and only the star's answers were saved on tape. Consequently, Miss Truman and Mr. Wallace would carry on a six-hour back-and-forth conversation with someone they often never met.

They called this system "stop-start" taping. The question is asked "live" into a microphone and the answer is played on a tape machine. It was a great trick. Everybody was fooled except the public. On the opening "Weekday" show Margaret Truman announced, "Our star companion for today is Eddie Fisher. Hi, Eddie!"

Eddie never answered. Eddie was caught in the tape machine at NBC's Radio Central.

One day Walter Kiernan said to Rosemary Clooney, "Did you and your sister Betty start in show business together?"

To which Miss Clooney replied: "I certainly do and so does Joe. It's the only way to raise children."

Economy wasn't the only problem "Weekday" had. The concept wasn't bad. The critics liked the show, but the radio plague was upon the networks, and nothing was working right. So "Weekday" ran just under a year.

Radio's Worst Hour

NBC replaced it with another "concept" show. This one was called "Bandstand."

This time the cry was "Damn the economics, and full speed ahead!"

Running from ten in the morning until noon, Monday through Friday, the program featured the music of the biggest, most famous, most glamorous dance bands in all the land.

Tommy and Jimmy Dorsey were signed. Xavier Cugat, Art Mooney, Skinnay Ennis, Freddy Martin, Tex Beneke, The Glenn Miller orchestra with Ray McKinley.

NBC was trying, again, the original concept.

When radio networks first came into existence they did so because they filled a need. Radio had become the prime source of entertainment. There were music, comedy, drama, and variety for the vast majority. Few stations could afford or were able physically to get the mixture of creative talents—performers, writers, directors, technicians —that were necessary for top programming in all these fields. The networks could do for the stations what they, individually, could not do for themselves in providing important programs of all kinds.

Now the shoe was on the station's foot.

With network programming withering on the vine, stations were doing well for themselves. The big soap and cigarette companies were discovering that hometown personalities were racking up higher ratings than network shows. National spot business was flowing into local outlets, and stations not only found that network programming was lacking; many also dropped their long-time affiliations with the big webs.

Ironically, the programming that local stations now

offered was called, at one time, "local fills"—recorded interludes between network shows.

The disc jockey had arrived and was taking over.

Independent stations were beginning to find themselves the lions in the arena where they had been the lambs.

The disc jockey started this amazing growth about 1940 when independent stations in big cities were successful in commanding a respectable share of the audience by using star-type personalities to play the recordings that were the stations' program foundation.

Martin Block, Fred Robbins, Stan Shaw, and Art Ford were typical of the big-time deejay who took the record show out of the local-fill category and gave it prominence.

By the time television was making great inroads as a novelty factor, something was happening in the music business.

Vaughn Monroe disbanded his orchestra and became a single. Woody Herman no longer toured the nation with his big aggregation. The soloist was coming into his own. Frank Sinatra, who had been a band singer, was now a hot solo property. Dick Haymes didn't need Harry James any'more.

The soloist prospered, and a single act could command record sales and personal-appearance money that heretofore had been the property of the big band. New soloists appeared . . . along with a new form of "music." Rock 'n' roll was rearing its ugly head.

The disc jockey was becoming more and more important to the music publisher and the record company, and the chaos that resulted led to some rather unpleasant things in radio.

One disc spinner who was riding the crest of the new

wave of popularity was Cleveland's Bill Randle. His ratings on WERE made him one of the most influential programmers in the country—and he had a salary to prove it.

Bill, who is now on WCBS in New York, had some pretty cogent things to say about what had happened at the local level all over the country.

"Radio is, of course, many things to many people," Randle says. "But a large number of radio stations today are involved in the grinding out of a rigidly limited list of mediocre, currently popular songs tightly interspersed with insistent and incessant commercials, superimposed on a blur of monomaniacal jingles, contests, weather reports, capsule news, meaningless salutes and gimmicks, and a hodgepodge of 'public service' announcements."

In the early days of the disc jockey, the personality selected his own music. Then came the revolution. Randle said:

"In the mid-fifties, with the growth of independent stations to an important position in the industry, a new force came into play. Chain operations came to the big cities with task forces of glib, fast-talking, low-paid announcers, hopped-up musical station identification, public-service jingles, slickly designed contests, and well-tested attention-getting gimmicks. Each had a rigid, all-inclusive music formula.

"Within a short time the 'new sound,' aided by aggressive promotion, skyrocketed to an important position in the industry. 'Top forty' and a new 'swingin' station' formula were shortly imitated and emulated by a large and ever-increasing number of stations. With the rise of formula radio, the position of the high-paid personality

disc jockeys became untenable, and many of these performers have now disappeared from the radio scene.

"In their place, almost totally devoid of any individual
personalities, many even with manufactured names owned
by the stations where they are employed, developed a
group of young announcers trained to repeat rapidly and
enthusiastically a highly limited and inane group of stock
phrases dealing with the time, weather, station identification, and music lists."

Why? First let's lay a little blame at the door of the
rating services. One of the most-used surveys is what is
known as a recall study—the "What were you doing last
night?" technique. People must remember in order to
report.

When programs per se left radio, there was only the
general sound left. Listeners no longer remembered the
programs they heard. In another era they could say, "I
listened to 'The Bob Hope Show' last night," or "I hear
Jack Benny every week," or "Fred Allen is my favorite
program."

As the big network show disappeared, many stations
felt they were dependent on call letters to get proper
identification in this rating service. So the station's call
letters went on the block like a pack of cigarettes.

Some stations changed their call letters to make them
easier to remember—if possible, to make them sound like
a word. KABL, KISN, WADO. Others adopted the idea
that if call letters were repeated often enough, there would
be tremendous "recall" value when the surveyor asked
"what station?"

So it became WXBS time, WXBS weather, WXBS

Radio's Worst Hour

Tune Number Five, WXBS, WXBS, WXBS, until it was used as much as the word "the."

When it was WXBS News, the listener heard it through an echo chamber, and there were sound effects of whistles, bells, teletypes, frequency tones.

There were shouting, mechanical-sounding catch-phrases, and nerve-jangling musical blasts.

It was the theory of "The Big Lie." Shout it often enough, and they can't forget.

Not only bad radio—terrible radio.

The only thing worse was the music.

Newspapers and magazines often reported the beginning of this kind of broadcasting with a story. It seems, the myth goes, that a radio station manager was having a coke in a teenage oasis. The jukebox was playing. The youngsters kept feeding dimes into the machine to hear a half-dozen rock 'n' roll numbers over and over again. As he watched the kids feed their cash into the box, he wondered if this wasn't the answer. Didn't these teenagers want to hear only a few "hits" over and over? What would happen if he programmed his station that way? A few dozen of the wildest, most popular records over and over and over? Why not?

Whether the story is true or not, radio stations in nearly every town seemed to be trying the theory.

Bill Randle went into *Variety* to ask some questions about this programming theory.

"Why do many stations continue to program a music formula that, to them, represents the lowest common denominator?" Randle asked.

"The answer that you will get from the managers and performers is 'We want to give the public what it wants!'

They say they're playing what they're buying—and if they don't play it somebody else will.

"These managers are convinced that the 'hot hundred' or the 'top forty' or the 'fabulous fifty,' primarily by teen-age artists, are essential to maintain a big audience in modern radio.

"Who really buys what in the highly diversified record market is a difficult question to answer. Despite research, there is really no consensus of opinion.

"The most acceptable statements are that subteens and teenagers buy most of the single popular records and that later teenagers and adults buy most of the albums. There is obviously an extensive overlap in most directions.

"Even if we accept the record-buying public as a true sample of the mass radio audience, we are faced with an unusual situation. Most recorded music sold through music stores and record clubs is of the album variety—and only a small part of it is remotely similar to the music that dominates the popular charts and formula music of radio broadcasting."

Then Bill asks the big question:

"If formula radio stations are playing 'what the public wants'—determined by the sales of phonograph records— why aren't they programming in a way that represents the actual economics of the record business?"

Bill's idea is that formula stations are programming what a small minority are purchasing, thinking "This is it."

So radio, in too many instances, became a background of music and noises interspersed with "service" announcements.

There seemed to be nothing left for the adults.

Radio's Worst Hour

Some radio stations seemed to have lost their dedication to do what their licenses called for—what people needed and wanted. Radio had panicked, and prostituted itself. It had become a secondary medium, a noise to have in the house when there was nothing much to watch on television.

A grim time.

CHAPTER 22

And So Tomorrow . . .

IN THE past thirty years, radio has been tied to the whipping post of every town square in the nation. And the whip has been vigorously applied by millions of people.

It was abused and criticized in its bright, energetic, creative beginnings; in its smug, fat, opulent golden days; and in its hectic, uncertain adjustment to television.

In the next decade radio will receive the same treatment from its critics. Yet it seems to us that radio has now found and accepted its unique but most important role both in broadcasting and in the social structure of the United States.

Broadcasters know and accept certain obvious facts. They realize that the networks and their affiliated stations will never again command a huge mass audience. This is TV's domain in the foreseeable future. They also know that no one station will completely meet the needs of our larger, more complex communities.

And So Tomorrow . . .

Stations, both network affiliates and independents, are deliberately programming for specialized audiences. This varies by age segments, by special interests, such as sports, news, or types of music; and by ethnic or language groups in metropolitan markets.

If a word fits radio today, it's "diversification." It's news, sports, and all kinds of music; it's talk, discussion, and participation; and it's entertainment and information.

The networks have adjusted their service to fit modern radio. First and foremost, they give their affiliates a fine, aggressive news service—news as it happens, plus excellent analysis and background. They offer wide coverage of special events, ranging from space shots at Cape Canaveral, UN sessions, direct reports from troubled Mississippi or the various capitals of the world. They broadcast public affairs and discussions, such as "Meet the Press" and "Capitol Cloakroom"; "Invitation to Learning"; live music ranging from the New York Philharmonic-Symphony to leading dance bands; and sports, such as Bowl Games, the World Series, and the Kentucky Derby. In addition, "Flair" (ABC), "Monitor" (NBC), and "Dimensions" (CBS) offer interesting and varied segmented programs on everything from Broadway to outer space.

Network programs fill on the average about 20 percent of the broadcast schedule of their affiliates. The type of service now offered is easily integrated into the full schedule, and permits the station to identify with its local community.

The independent stations are equally aware that the whole context of listening to radio has changed, and are adjusting their programming accordingly.

It Sounds Impossible

Broadcasters know that "out of home listening" will increase each year. Those sixty million sets (cars, small shops, and portable transistors) will probably double over the next decade. Radio more and more is becoming an all-day companion that goes everywhere, anyplace, anytime. It is becoming a portable news ticker, a traveling music hall, a roving conversationalist, an itinerant spectator of sporting events.

As radio grows in size with its new mobility, it still retains many of its most powerful old characteristics. It can still move with greater speed and directness than any other medium. It can cover more of this country and the world. It can still reach into more homes (fifty million today, most of them with two or more sets) and get there quicker.

Radio can certainly provide its growing audience, better and faster than any competitor, with companionable music, news, and information.

Superb advances in recording, playback techniques, and equipment have put excellent music of all kinds within the reach of every radio station. About the only limitation in presenting music is the individual judgment and taste of the broadcaster. This is particularly true with the introduction of stereophonic FM and the rapid growth of FM stations in the last few years.

Radio still has the ability to make news available at almost the instant it happens. Newspapers and magazines may be able to give more background, different viewpoints, and greater depth, and TV offers pictorial treatment, if it can get cameras to the site, or film back. But only radio can transmit instantly from anywhere, at any time of day or night.

Broadcasters realize that we live in a time of rapidly

moving, exciting events about which its listeners want to be informed quickly, reliably, and interestingly. Radio has quickly accepted this responsibility, and in the field of informational programming it is giving its audience far more than hard news and special events. Radio provides informed analysis on a wide variety of subjects, explores special news areas, such as science, business, education, and so on; it offers profiles and sidelights on personalities, and does "specials" on events ranging from an Indian War to presidential press conferences. All this is done on a local, state, national, and international level.

Electronic journalism today has its own special problems that must be solved as broadcasters seek to find fuller and wiser uses of both radio and TV in the news field.

Today radio and TV are flatly prohibited by a rule of the House of Representatives from bringing public hearings of its committees to the American people. They are prohibited generally by rulings stemming from Canon 35 of the American Bar Association from bringing open sessions of the courts to the American people.

"Both these situations are unreasonable anachronisms," said William S. Paley, CBS Board Chairman, recently.

"Hearing chambers and courtrooms closed to direct coverage by major news media are wholly inconsistent with the democratic objective of an informed people," he continued. "In this day of quiet, inconspicuous broadcasting equipment, it is ridiculous to say that these sessions can be open to anybody that can crowd into the room, but must be closed to everyone else who would witness the proceedings, or reveal excerpts of them through broadcasting. All of us . . . in broadcasting and outside . . . ought to fight this stubborn and pointless discrimination in every way we can until it goes the way of every other survival of the dark ages."

A headache kindred to Canon 35 is Section 315 of the Federal Communications Act of 1934 which, in effect, denies vital political information to the American people. Generally known as the "equal time law," Section 315 states that a broadcaster who gives or sells time to a political candidate must be prepared to give or sell equal time to any and every legally qualified rival candidate. Under this section, broadcasters cannot offer free time to major candidates without opening themselves to a group of equal-time demands from splinter groups and even crackpots.

The National Association of Broadcasters, the networks, a vast majority of stations, and even certain members of the FCC are now seeking repeal or modification of this section. Most broadcasters say it should be eliminated completely because it's an artificial brake preventing the industry from doing the best possible job. If broadcasters do a poor job, they point out, they will hear loudly and clearly from the press, the politicians, and the people. With this we agree completely.

The industry argues, with great justification, that, since given the right to editorialize, it has effectively and responsibly discharged this obligation. As there have been great confusion and controversy over the right to editorialize, a quick review seems pertinent.

In 1941 the FCC was asked to renew the license of station WAAB, owned by the Mayflower Broadcasting Corporation. The station had previously broadcast editorials urging the election of certain candidates and supporting issues favored by the station's owners. The station was openly entering into controversy in its own name, just as hundreds of stations are doing today.

In its renewal application, the station promised it would broadcast no more editorials, and the license was granted. The FCC decision said in part: "This licensee has revealed a serious misconception of its duties and functions under the law. A truly free radio cannot be used to advocate the causes of the licensee. It cannot be used to support the candidates of its friends. It cannot be devoted to the support of principles it happens to regard most favorably. In brief, the broadcaster cannot be an advocate."

For years, the broadcasters fought this ruling. The NAB called it a gross example of the FCC's encroachment upon free speech. In 1949 the FCC revoked its ban against editorials but urged the broadcaster to take affirmative steps to seek out and present opposing views.

The growth of editorializing was slow during the first few years. Broadcasters had to find their way and develop their own techniques. They had to build confidence, for it takes courage to stand up and be counted.

In the last few years the practice has expanded rapidly. Today over half the stations in the nation are doing some editorializing; most of the others have plans to start in the immediate future, according to an NAB survey in 1962.

This taking of positions by stations (mostly in radio) in hundreds of American communities is a healthy development. Throughout most of our history, choices and conflicting viewpoints were presented by the newspapers. The country grew and prospered, undoubtedly helped by prodding and controversy in the years when there were several dailies in each major city.

The postwar years have seen a drastic reduction in daily newspapers. Forty years ago, 522 cities had competing newspapers. Today there are only 55 such cities. In 23 states, there is not a single city with competitive newspapers. Since 1952, 20 metropolitan dailies have merged, folded, or become weeklies. In the same decade, not a single new daily has been successfully established in a city with over 500,000 population.

This left a tremendous vacuum, which is being filled to some extent by radio and TV, both in reporting the news in depth and in editorializing about it.

Editorials certainly help make a station an integral part of community life. The actual process of putting an editorial on the air, of sifting through problems, of taking a point of view, of substantiating it with facts, and of giving the other side a chance to tell you and the public how wrong he thinks you are, requires judgment, tact, and responsibility.

Broadcasters believe their record in this most sensitive area is a valid argument for the repeal of court and committee restrictions and of the equal-time "law."

While programs will definitely be a major factor in the future of broadcasting, another factor, little discussed or thought about by the average listener, will possibly be of equal importance. That is the actual sound of radio as you hear it on your receiving set.

Back in the twenties, the actual sound produced by the receiver was, to contemporary conditioned ears, absolutely unacceptable. Static was a major problem. There were hundreds of other interruptive sounds that made listening difficult. Yet millions listened, and enjoyed what they heard. The reason for this identification with minimum aural pleasure is simple: an innovation with tremendous impact made the novelty of the experience overcome any hearing handicap. The only comparable instruments then were the telephone and the phonograph. Pre-electric recording wasn't much better than radio, and it was considerably more expensive as a leisure activity. In addition, radio was new; people were talking about it; and listening to it . . . was the thing to do.

Even in those early days it became clear that physical sound in itself can often be an important factor in listening habits. And *sound* today is far more important with the coming of television.

People say today, in answer to questionnaires or researchers, "I like the sound of that station," or, "It has such a pleasant sound," or, "I hate rock 'n' roll," "Pretty music appeals to me," or "Teenage music has too loud a beat."

Most of us can adjust to any sound, except a painfully disturbing one. And from a psychological point of view, there is no musical sound, once a frame of reference has been established, that cannot produce pleasure. Almost any style of music, presented in a positive and prestigeful way, can be given status and acceptability by any individual in our society, regardless of age, economic status, musical skill, or social background. In this way even the crudest of Negro music, white southern country music, and western music, primitive religious music or atonal classical music can be given the highest acceptability within an intellectual segment of the community.

In the same way, a peculiar synthesis of Negro, folk,

and regular popular music has evolved out of the economics of the music industry, melding together highly antagonistic social and economic groups into a huge mass audience.

This audience has been largely catered to by the independent stations and has assumed a most important position in the industry. The single most important factor in this dominance has been the focusing of status "by numbers" tagged on the particular pieces of popular music played by the stations.

Analyze the symbols "top forty" or "going by the numbers," and you find that these stations constantly use superlatives, in a dynamic and positive way, in introducing records: Number One! Smash! The best! The greatest! Top hit! The Champ! Sure best seller! Winner! Such words and phrases have been constants for years in this type of radio operation. Such conditioning over the years has resulted in the belief within the industry that these stations really do play the most popular music; and the listener, persuaded by constant and blatant promotion, believes that he is listening to music preferred by a vast majority of the people.

Remember, too, that almost all programming material used on these stations is distributed free of charge by the record companies. The stations for the most part reflect only what is produced by the record companies, which is certainly not a true reflection of public taste in America.

Program executives, in attempting future planning, must take into consideration the following trends and facts:

More and more people are using radio as a background

medium for work. What kind of programming is interesting yet doesn't interfere with routine?

Population statistics forecast a tremendous growth in young and older people in the next fifteen years, with a significant drop in the middle-age range.

The migration of southern Negroes and Puerto Ricans is pouring millions of non-whites into northern urban areas. How does radio meet their tastes and demands without offending its regular listeners?

Automation is creating a large number of permanently unemployed, and untrained workers will add millions more to this group by 1970.

Shorter working hours will add extensive leisure time to the average worker's day and will greatly increase his mobility.

As urban areas spread (Boston to Washington in ten years will be almost a continuing city), village and small-town loyalties and interest will be diluted. Communities will have to expand to cover multicity and county areas with considerable political service and social blending.

More and more radio will be mobile (small transistors as well as automobiles) and must compete with outside environment and higher noise levels.

After analyzing these facts, and talking with scores of broadcasters, here is our blueprint for the next decade:

First of all, the sound level will be higher. This has been accomplished on a crude level to date by an increase in gain, the playing of hotter records (with juiced-up sound), the use of echo chambers and other electronic devices. Since loudness and intensity are major factors to the listener, many stations will use such terms as "enhanced sound" to justify, give prestige to, and validate their operation. Actually, this loudness can be masked in such a way that the listener never really knows that it is happening, and it enables the station to compete against the increased environmental sounds that are increasingly present in urban society.

The pacing of radio stations will be faster, either mechanically induced or through the increased flow of communication. The American rate of speech is now considerably faster than it was in 1950. Such increases in normal speech are usually followed by an increase on the part of the professional communicator. As our pattern of life speeds up, the communicator who dawdles, drags out the sentence, plays the lingering melody too often, will fall by the wayside.

You can expect much greater diversification of programs. There will be more news in depth, more documentaries on social and economic problems, more forum, interviews and discussions, and far more editorials. Use of the telephone where the audience is encouraged to express opinions on current affairs, or to get advice and information from experts (doctors, lawyers, clergy, fashion experts, critics, decorators, and so on), will increase. Sports will extend beyond baseball, football, and basketball, and cover many secondary contests.

There will be few if any dramatic programs, primarily because of economic reasons. There will be an even greater interest in international broadcasting, and many more exchange programs.

Radio stations know they have to reflect the community in which they live, adequately and intelligently, to survive and grow. Besides reflecting the real, and felt, and at times even the unconscious needs of the community, the station must be a strong force for social, economic, and cultural growth.

Radio, in this age of mass production, education, government, and communications, will, we think, adjust itself to the demands and opportunities of the future.

Even if it sounds impossible.

Index

Index

Index

Index

Index

Index

Index

Index

Index

Index

Network broadcasting, 59-69, 157-62
first "network," 60
in Great Britain, 94-95
MBS formed 158-59
percentage of affiliates' schedules filled by, 243
Yankee Network, 195
See also American Broadcasting Company; Columbia Broadcasting System; National Broadcasting Company
Nelson, Ozzie, 77
New Deal, 205
New York, N.Y., *see* WABC; WBAY; WCBS; WEAF; WHN; WJZ; WMCA; WMGM; WNBC; WOR; WRCA
New York Philharmonic-Symphony, 225, 243
Newark, N.J., *see* WJZ; WOR
Newfoundland, Marconi in, xii-xiii
Newman, H. H., 66
News, 182-211, 244-45
birth of radio news, 8
Columbia News Service, 189-95
Press-Radio Bureau, 194-95
See also Documentary programs; Politics; Special Events
Newspapers
decline in competitive, 248
oppose radio news, 189-90
Niel (Godfrey's chauffeur), 1, 216
Nielson, A. C., Company, 227
Nixon-Kennedy debates, 198-99, 210
"Nussbaum, Mrs.," 121

Oakie, Jack, 59
Ochs, Adolf, 42
Ogden, Utah, KLO, 43
Ohio State Penitentiary fire, 41
O'Keefe, Walter, viii
Old Gold Cigarettes, 159
Olsen George, 64
"Operas in English," 86, 119
"Original Good Will Hour, The," 131, 133-34

"Orphan Annie," 142-43, 168
"Our Gal Sunday," 173-74, 177
Ovaltine, 144

Paar, Jack, 1, 216
Paley, William Samuel, 157
buys CBS, 68-69
on Canon 35, 245-46
competes with NBC, 78-81
as president of CBS, 159-60, 161-162
Palmolive Shave Cream, 159
Panel-quiz shows, 5
Paramount-Publix Corporation, 69
Parker, Seth, *see* Lord, Phillips H.
Parks, Bert, viii, 1, 231
"Parkyakarkus," 117
Pathé "talking machine," 7
Pearl, Jack, 139-40
Penner, Joe, 77, 139
"Pennsylvania Six-Five-Thousand,"4
"Pennyfeather, Mrs.," 129
Pepsi-Cola, 140
Perfect Fool, The (play), broadcast of, 30-31
"Perfect Song, The," 166
Peterson, Curt, 114
Philadelphia, Pa., WIP, 41
Phillips, Sandra, 43
Pickard, Sam, 68-69
Pickford, Mary, 31, 111
Pious, Minerva, 120
Pittsburgh, Pa., *see* KDKA
Pius XI, Pope, inaugurates Vatican City station, 41
Politics and radio, 197-211
editorials on candidates, 246-47
"fireside chats," 198, 202, 203-04
first broadcast of election returns, 15, 199
first broadcast of national conventions, 200-1
"equal time law," 207, 209-11, 246
Nixon-Kennedy debates, 198-99, 210

Index

Index

Index

Index

Index

Index

WRC (Washington, D.C.)
  broadcasts memorial services for Harding, 41
  broadcasts opening of Congress, 200
WRCA (New York, N.Y.), 18
Writtle, England, 90
WTAM (Cleveland, Ohio), 71, 77
WWJ (Detroit, Mich.), 18
Wylie, Max
  describes "Strike It Rich," 135

Wylie, Max—(Contd.)
  on psychology of soap operas, 171-172
Wynn, Ed, 31, 119, 139
  in broadcast of *The Perfect Fool*, 30-31

Yankee Network, 195
Young and Rubicam (advertising agency), 87